MAUI TRAVEL BOOK 2023

The Updated guide on where to go, what to see, and do for first timers in Maui and beyond.

Jay Garrett

Copyright © 2023 Jay Garrett

All rights reserved. No part of this publication may be reproduced, distributed, or transmitted in any form or by any means, including photocopying, recording, or other electronic or mechanical methods, without the prior written permission of the publisher, except in the case of brief quotations embodied in critical reviews and certain other noncommercial uses permitted by copyright law.

TABLE OF CONTENTS

INTRODUCTION 9
CHAPTER ONE 12
    Overview of Maui 13
    A Brief History of Maui 15
    Location of Maui 18
    Weather in Maui 20
CHAPTER TWO 23
    When to visit Maui 23
    Getting to Maui 25
    How to navigate Maui 27
    Accommodations in Maui 29
    Packing list for Maui 31
CHAPTER THREE 35
    Top Attractions in Maui 35
    Road to Hana 35
    National Park of Haleakala 37
    Lahaina 39

Beach at Kaanapali 41

Crater of Molokani 43

Park Iao Valley State 45

Ocean Center in Maui 47

Botanical Garden of Kula 49

Hawaii Bay 51

CHAPTER FOUR 55

Outdoor Activities in Maui 55

CHAPTER FIVE 59

Best beaches in Maui 59

Family-friendly beaches 61

Beaches with coral reefs 63

Beaches with surfboards 64

Beaches with no-clothing policies 66

CHAPTER SIX 69

Traditional Hawaiian cuisine 69

Maui's top restaurants 71

Breweries and distilleries in the area 74

Farmers' markets and food trucks 77

CHAPTER SEVEN 81

    Bars and clubs in Maui 81

    Nightlife in Maui 81

    Concert venues 83

    Cultural festivals and luaus 85

CHAPTER EIGHT 89

    Shopping in Maui 89

    Local markets and boutiques 89

    Gifts and mementos 91

    Attractive stores in Wailea 93

CHAPTER NINE 97

    Wellness and Spa in Maui - Yoga and meditation . 97

    Massages and spa services 99

    Outdoor exercises for health 102

CHAPTER TEN 105

    Best family-friendly attractions 105

    Family-friendly beaches 107

Activities for kids and teens 109

CHAPTER ELEVEN 113

LGBTQ+ Maui - LGBTQ+ friendly activities and events 113

Gay clubs and bars 115

LGBTQ+-friendly facilities 117

CHAPTER TWELVE. 121

Sustainable Tourism in Maui - Eco-tourism in Maui 121

Responsible travel practices 124

Supporting local communities and businesses 126

CHAPTER THIRTEEN 131

Cultural Maui - Hawaiian cultural events and festivals 131

Historical sites and museums 134

Traditional arts and crafts 136

CHAPTER FOURTEEN. 140

Road Trips in Maui - West Maui Loop 141

Upcountry Maui 143

South Maui Drive 146

East Maui Drive 148

CHAPTER FIFTEEN. 151

Off-the-Beaten-Path in Maui - Hidden beaches and waterfalls 151

Secret hikes and trails 153

Unique cultural experiences 155

CHAPTER SIXTEEN. 158

Maui for Adventure Seekers - Extreme sports and activities 159

CHAPTER SEVENTEEN 162

Maui for Romance - Romantic activities and attractions 163

Best locations for a honeymoon 166

Intimate dining experiences 167

Private Chef Experience 168

Dinner cruise at dusk 168

Farm-to-Table Dining 169

Experience at the Chef's Table 169

CHAPTER EIGHTEEN 170

   Maui for Solo Travelers Solo - friendly activities and events... 171

   Social and networking opportunities 174

   Safety tips for solo travelers 177

   Advice on safety for lone travelers 179

CHAPTER NINTEEN. 183

   Events and Festivals in Maui - Maui Film Festival 183

   Maui County Fair 185

   Maui Marathon 190

CHAPTER TWENTY 195

   Travel Tips for Maui - Money-saving tips 197

   Safety and health tips 200

INTRODUCTION

Aloha, friends!

Are you ready to embark on a tropical adventure to Maui, the land of sun, sea, and surf? Well, hold on to your flip-flops because I've got a hilarious story to share with you!

Once upon a time, there was a tourist named Tom who decided to explore the beautiful island of Maui. He had read all the guidebooks and thought he knew everything there was to know about the island.

However, on his first day, he made a rookie mistake and didn't apply sunscreen before hitting the beach. Little did he know, the Maui sun is no joke, and he ended up with a gnarly sunburn that turned him into a walking lobster. But that's not even the funniest part!

Tom was so desperate for relief that he stumbled upon a local remedy: rubbing himself with fresh aloe vera straight from the plant.

He thought he had found the ultimate cure, but there was just one problem... he accidentally picked a cactus instead of an aloe vera plant!

Needless to say, Tom's Maui adventure was off to a bumpy start, but he soon learned the ins and outs of the island with the help of his trusty guidebook.

From snorkeling with sea turtles to hiking to hidden waterfalls, he discovered all the best spots to make the most of his vacation.

So, if you don't want to end up like poor Tom, make sure to grab a copy of our Maui travel guidebook. It's chock-full of useful tips, fun stories, and breathtaking photos that will help you plan the trip of a lifetime.

And who knows, you might even discover your own hilarious adventure along the way!

CHAPTER ONE

Overview of Maui

The second-largest Hawaiian island, Maui, is in the Pacific Ocean's center. It is a well-liked vacation spot renowned for its natural beauty, beaches, and outdoor pursuits, including hiking, surfing, and snorkeling. Many plants and animals, including rare ones unique to Maui, can be found there.

Each of the regions that make up Maui has its distinct qualities. Famous beaches like Kaanapali and Lahaina and opulent resorts may be found along the west coast.

The renowned Haleakala volcano on the south coast is a well-liked hiking and cycling attraction. The less developed east coast is famous for its waterfalls and lush forests. Maui has a sizable Native Hawaiian population and a rich history and culture.

Many historic Hawaiian sites, including petroglyphs and heiau (holy temples), can be found on the island (rock carvings). Tourists may learn about Hawaiian culture through diverse activities, including hula lessons, lei-making workshops, and traditional luaus.

The primary sources of revenue for Maui's economy are travel and tourism, particularly from the United States, Canada, and Japan. Agriculture used to be a key business on the island, producing sugar cane and pineapples, but it has recently decreased.

With several biotechnology, software, and renewable energy businesses, Maui is also home to a developing technological sector. Maui is a stunning and distinctive location with plenty to offer everyone.

It has everything you might want, from a leisurely beach getaway to an outdoor activity.

It is a must-visit location for everyone visiting Hawaii because of its natural beauty, vibrant culture, and kind people.

A Brief History of Maui

The first Polynesian immigrants arrived in Maui more than a thousand years ago, beginning the island's history. The island's history would be shaped for centuries by these early immigrants' culture, language, and customs.

The Hawaiian island of Maui was divided into several chiefdoms, each headed by a strong chief known as an **alibi**. These leaders managed the land, water, and other resources, keeping peace and resolving conflicts within their community.

The introduction of European explorers and traders in the late 18th century profoundly affected Maui's history. The Spanish were the first Europeans to come to the island in the sixteenth century, albeit they only stayed there briefly. The island was later visited by British explorer James Cook in the late 18th century, who named it "Sandwich Islands" in tribute to the Earl of Sandwich.

Trade and commerce expanded quickly during this period, and the entrance of whaling ships resulted in a large influx of sailors, merchants, and other foreigners on the island. As a result, Lahaina became a significant port and trading hub, with traders from all over the world conducting business there.

Maui was one of the final islands brought under the dominion of Hawaiian King Kamehameha I, who started his drive to unite the islands under his rule in 1795.

It took Kamehameha several years to overthrow the island's solid chiefs and establish his practice due to the severe competition for Maui.

With numerous plantations created on the island, Maui developed into a significant hub for the production of sugar cane and pineapples in the 19th century. This resulted in an inflow of labor immigrants from nations like China, Japan, and the Philippines, who significantly impacted Maui's history and culture.

With numerous airfields and naval installations built on the island during World War II, Maui was a significant military facility crucial to the war effort. After the war, Maui's natural beauty, beaches, and outdoor activities drew tourists worldwide. Tourism grew in importance as a business.

With a diverse population and a distinct past honored and preserved via various cultural events and activities, Maui is still a thriving and culturally rich destination today.

Location of Maui

Hawaii's Central Pacific contains the island of Maui. Hawaii's second-largest island has a surface area of 727.2 square miles. Maui is a volcanic island member of the Hawaiian Island group. It features a varied landscape, including lush jungles, imposing mountains, immaculate beaches, and dry deserts.

The dormant Haleakala volcano on the Hawaiian island of Maui rises to 10,023 feet and is one of the island's most spectacular geological features. Haleakal's peak is a well-liked location for hikers and stargazers alike, and it provides a spectacular view of the nearby islands. One of the world's largest volcanic craters, Haleakal, is more than 7 miles long, 2 miles broad, and 2,600 feet deep.

The West Maui Mountains, a collection of peaks that reach a height of 5,788 feet, are another feature of the Hawaiian island of Maui.

Due to its rocky terrain and high cliffs, the West Maui Mountains is a well-liked destination for hikers and adventurers.

Maui's hilly landscape is complemented by several stunning beaches, notably Kaanapali Beach, one of the island's busiest beaches. Wailea Beach, Napili Bay, and Kapalua Bay are a few other renowned beaches on the island of Maui.

These beaches have spectacular views of the Pacific Ocean, white sand, and crystal blue water. The lush woods that cover a large portion of the island's eastern slopes are another aspect of Maui's geography that stands out.

Visitors who want to explore the island's jungles, waterfalls, and breathtaking panoramas frequently travel the Hana Highway, which hugs Maui's eastern coast.

Overall, visitors can explore and take in Maui's diversified geography, which presents a singular and beautiful backdrop. Whether you like hiking, surfing, or relaxing on the beach, Maui has something to offer everyone.

Weather in Maui

Maui experiences a tropical environment with moderate temperatures and sunshine all year. The island's location in Hawaii's Central Pacific region and the trade winds that blow over the island from the northeast significantly impact the island's weather.

On Maui, the weather is generally consistent throughout the year, with daytime highs typically in the mid-to low-70s Fahrenheit (23-28 degrees Celsius). Average evening temperatures range from the mid-60s to the low-70s Fahrenheit (15-21 degrees Celsius). The elevation and time of day, however, can affect the temperature.

Two distinct seasons—a wet season and a dry season—define Maui's climate. The island experiences a more significant amount of rainfall and a drop in temperature during the rainy season, which lasts from **November to March.**

The trade winds bring moisture to the island during this season, which causes a lot of rain showers and a gloomy sky. Mountainous locations experience the highest rainfall during this time, which can cause landslides and flash flooding.

From **April through October,** the dry season is in full swing, characterized by bright, sunny days with low humidity and minimal rainfall. Although the trade winds are usually more robust at this time, the temperature and air quality is kept at a comfortable level. Nevertheless, one of the most alluring aspects of Maui is its environment, which boasts comfortable temperatures and sunny skies for much of the year.

Nonetheless, tourists should be ready for the occasional downpour, especially during the rainy season. A lightweight raincoat or umbrella is always a good option, especially if you intend to explore the island's mountainous sections.

CHAPTER TWO

When to visit Maui

The best time to visit Maui depends on your interests and what you want to do while you're there. Maui is a well-known tourist destination for visitors from all over the world.

Mid-December through mid-April, when many American schools are on winter break, marks Maui's busiest travel period. The island may be somewhat congested during this time, and lodging, entertainment, and travel costs are likely higher.

If you visit Maui during the busiest time of year, you can book your accommodation and activities well in advance. Maui may be visited at its best during the shoulder seasons of May to mid-June and September to mid-December. The weather is still pleasant and sunny at these times, but fewer visitors are on the island.

Thus lodging costs and activity costs may be reduced. Because the ocean is warm, these times are ideal for participating in water sports like swimming, snorkeling, and surfing.

Consider traveling to Maui from **mid-June to August** to find the best deals and the least number of tourists. Schools are out for the summer, and many families are traveling. It's essential to remember that this time of year can have hotter and more humid weather, as well as sporadic afternoon rains.

Whenever you decide to travel to Maui, there will always be many fun things to do and see. Maui has activities for everyone, whether hiking, surfing, whale watching, or just lounging on the beach. Just be sure to check the forecast and make travel plans by it. Furthermore, remember to pack lots of sunscreens and a hat to protect yourself from the intense Hawaiian sun.

Getting to Maui

Depending on your location and financial situation, there are various ways to get to Maui, a well-liked vacation spot. Here are a few possibilities:

Air: Kahului Airport (OGG), the island's primary airport, is the most popular way to travel to Maui. Direct flights from several major cities in the United States, Canada, and other countries are available to Maui. To travel to your hotel or other locations on the island after landing at Kahului Airport, you can hire a car, use a shuttle or cab, or use the island's public transit system.

Cruise Ship: Traveling to Maui by cruise ship is an additional alternative. You can tour Maui while taking advantage of the comforts and entertainment on board one of the several major cruise lines' itineraries, including stops there. Typically, cruise ships dock at Lahaina Harbor, from whence you can take a shuttle or a taxi to other island areas.

Ferry: Access between the islands of Maui and Lanai is made possible by the Maui-Lanai Expeditions ferry. It takes the ferry roughly 45 minutes to get from Lahaina Port to Lanai. This might be an enjoyable way to discover both islands and enjoy the beautiful Pacific Ocean scenery.

Island hopping is an option if you're considering visiting several islands in Hawaii. Inter-island flights are provided by several airlines, including Hawaiian Airlines and Mokulele Airlines. Flights take about 20 minutes to an hour, depending on the distance between the islands.

No matter your mode of transportation, it's crucial to make travel and lodging arrangements well in advance, especially during the busiest time of year for tourists. Maui is a place that is worth the journey because of its breathtaking beauty, comfortable climate, and wealth of activities.

How to navigate Maui

Hawaii's Maui is a stunning island with many unique spots to visit. You must determine the most effective means of transportation if you intend to visit Maui. To get about Maui, you have the following options:

Hiring a Car: Maui's most well-liked mode of transportation is a rental car. At the Kahului Airport or other locations throughout the island, renting a car is simple. Renting a car allows you to explore Maui at your leisure because the island has a strong network of highways. There are numerous vehicle rental agencies in Maui, so research costs and reserve early to get the best offers.

Using the Bus: The Maui Bus is the island of Maui's public transportation system. If you're on a tight budget, the bus service is a beautiful choice because it serves most of the island. The bus ticket is reasonable, and if you intend to take the bus frequently throughout the day, you can get a day pass.

Plan your trip appropriately, as the bus service can be sluggish and sporadic.

Renting a Taxi: Maui has taxi services, although they can be pricey. If you intend to use a cab, haggle the fare before getting in the vehicle. Alternatively, you might utilize one of the ride-hailing services offered on Maui, such as Uber or Lyft.

Biking: If you want to experience Maui's natural beauty up close, biking is a terrific way to get around. On Maui, you can rent a bike for a day or longer from one of the many bike rental businesses there. Due to the island's mountainous topography and busy highways, riding might be difficult, so correctly plan your route.

Walking is a fantastic choice if you are staying in a central location in Maui. Several sights and eateries are nearby, and walking is a convenient way to exercise and take in the island's stunning beauty.

Accommodations in Maui

Hawaii's Maui island is stunning, and many different types of lodging exist. There are many places to stay in Maui, whether you're looking for a five-star resort, an affordable hotel, or a vacation rental. Some of the top places to stay on the island are listed below:

Lahaina: On Maui's west coast, there is a historic town called Lahaina. Beautiful beaches, a buzzing nightlife, and art galleries are some of its top attractions. Lahaina has various hotels and rental homes, with prices ranging from cheap to luxurious.

Kaanapali: On Maui's northwest coast is the resort community of Kaanapali. Some of the island's most stunning beaches and opulent resorts can be found there. Kaanapali is an excellent place to stay if you want a leisurely beach holiday.

Kihei: Kihei is a town on Maui's southern coast. It is renowned for its lovely beaches and inexpensive lodging. Kihei is an excellent destination for vacationers on a tight budget because of the abundance of hotels, condos, and vacation rentals.

Wailea: On Maui's southern shore, there is a resort area called Wailea. It's renowned for its opulent resorts, top-notch golf courses, and breathtaking beaches. Wailea is the ideal destination if you want to have a luxurious vacation.

Hana: Hana is a tiny settlement on Maui's east coast. It is well-known for its pristine beaches, waterfalls, and thick rainforest. Hana is a terrific choice if you're searching for a serene getaway.

Upcountry Maui: The interior of the island's rural Upcountry Maui region. The area is renowned for its stunning landscape, which includes rolling hills, farms, and ranches. Upcountry Maui is a terrific spot to stay if you want an experience more off the beaten path.

Packing list for Maui

Prepare sensibly for the island's tropical heat and outdoor activities if you're considering visiting Maui. During your trip to Maui, you should carry the following items:

Lightweight Clothes: Due to Maui's warm, tropical climate, light clothes are a need. Bring shorts, t-shirts, tank tops, sundresses, and sandals for casual attire. Consider bringing a lightweight jacket or sweater for chilly evenings.

Swimwear is a must-pack item because Maui is home to some of the world's most breathtaking beaches. Bring a few swimsuits, a beach towel, and a cover-up.

Sun protection: The sun in Maui may be powerful, so bring a lot of sunscreens. Pack a high-SPF sunscreen, sunglasses, a hat, and a long-sleeved shirt or cover-up to shield your skin from the sun's harmful rays.

Hiking Shoes: Pack some good hiking shoes to trek or enjoy the island's natural beauty. Before your vacation, break in your shoes to prevent blisters and discomfort.

Water Shoes: Although Maui's beaches are stunning, several have rocky or irregular topography. Bring water shoes or sandals with a high grip to protect your feet and avoid falls.

Snorkeling equipment: Consider bringing your snorkeling equipment since Maui offers some of the best snorkeling in the world. You can rent equipment on the island if you have not had any.

Bug Repellent: Although Maui is not known for having a lot of mosquitoes, you might come across other insects like sand flies. Carry bug repellent to guard against stings and bites.

Reusable Water Bottle: Because Maui's tap water is safe, think about carrying one to keep hydrated while visiting the island. On the island, there are few locations with accessible bottle-filling facilities.

Bring Extra Cash: While most establishments in Maui take credit cards, it's a good idea to bring extra cash with you for little purchases or gratuities, even if most locations do.

In conclusion, you should take light clothing, swimwear, sun protection, hiking shoes, water shoes, snorkeling equipment, insect repellant, a reusable water bottle, cash, and credit cards for your trip to Maui. If you have these necessities, you'll be prepared to take advantage of all that Maui offers.

CHAPTER THREE

Top Attractions in Maui

Road to Hana

One of Hawaii's top tourist attractions is the gorgeous drive known as "The Road to Hana," located on Maui island. The 64.4-mile-long road meanders past flowing waterfalls, rocky coastlines, and verdant tropical rainforests. The trip may take two to four hours, depending on how many stops you make.

On Maui's north shore, the route starts in the town of Paia and travels eastward to the settlement of Hana. You will pass by some of the most stunning and desolate landscapes in the world as well as incredible vistas of the Pacific Ocean along the way. Not for the faint of heart, the route is twisty and narrow, with over 600 turns and 59 one-lane bridges.

You want to make sure to take all of the stops that are along the way. The first stop is Ho'okipa Beach Park, a well-liked location for kiteboarding and windsurfing. The picturesque town of Paia, which has a variety of stores and eateries, is accessible from there.

As you continue driving down the road, you will come across Twin Falls, an excellent swimming place. The Garden of Eden Arboretum and Botanical Garden, which boasts over 700 varieties of plants and flowers, is another place you can go.

The Waianapanapa State Park, one of the most well-liked pit breaks along the Road to Hana, has a black sand beach, lava caverns, and breathtaking ocean vistas. Moreover, you can go to Wailua Falls, an 80-foot-tall waterfall that falls into a pool below.

Hana is a peaceful little town with a storied past and vibrant culture. To learn more about the town's history, stop by the Hana Culture Center and

Museum, or wander inside the over-a-century-old Hasegawa General Store.

Anyone visiting Maui should take advantage of the Road to Hana. You will always remember this journey because of the breathtaking scenery, charming waterfalls, and cultural encounters. Remember to take it slow, be careful, and enjoy the trip.

National Park of Haleakala

On the Hawaiian island of Maui, there is a lovely and distinctive national park called Haleakala National Park. The park spans over 33,000 acres and is home to a dormant volcano, grand vistas, and unique ecosystems unmatched worldwide.

The Haleakala Crater, the park's centerpiece, is one of its primary attractions. This enormous depression in the ground was created by millions of years of volcanic activity, and it is now a well-liked vacation spot for travelers who come to walk, ride, and explore its strange terrain. More than 10,000 feet above sea level, Haleakala's summit offers panoramic views of the Pacific Ocean and the other islands.

The Haleakala Silversword, a rare plant that can only be found on the volcano's slopes, is one of the park's many distinctive ecosystems. One of the most well-known plants in the garden, the Silversword is distinguished by its unique silver leaves and gorgeous purple flowers. The Maui parrotbill, Hawaiian petrel, and Hawaiian goose are among the more endemic species that live in the park.

Haleakala National Park has a rich cultural heritage and natural beauty. The park has several historic Hawaiian landmarks, including temples, shrines, and other revered locations. With guided tours, exhibits, and other educational initiatives, tourists can learn about the history and culture of the Hawaiian people.

Haleakala National Park is a must-visit location for anybody traveling to Maui, whether they come to hike, explore, or take in the gorgeous landscape. It is undoubtedly one of the most remarkable national parks in the world because of its distinctive ecosystems, rich cultural heritage, and breathtaking natural beauty.

Lahaina

In Maui, Hawaii's west coast, there lies a quaint seaside community called Lahaina. Known for its rich history, breathtaking beaches, and exciting nightlife, Lahaina was once a thriving whaling community in the 19th century. Nowadays, it is a well-liked tourist attraction.

The historic district in Lahaina, home to several well-preserved structures from the town's early days as a whaling port, is one of its main draws. The Lahaina Courthouse, the Wo Hing Museum, and other notable sites can be seen in a walking tour of the neighborhood.

The stunning beaches of Lahaina are a further draw. There are several opportunities for sunbathing, swimming, and snorkeling, from the white sands of Ka'anapali Beach to the sapphire seas of Napili Bay. Lahaina's beaches are a great place to practice water sports like windsurfing and surfing.

Lahaina is renowned for having vibrant nightlife. The town's main artery, Front Street, has eateries, bars, and nightclubs that stay open late and provide live music, dancing, and other entertainment. Fleetwood's on Front Street, a restaurant and pub run by Fleetwood Mac legend Mick Fleetwood, is one of the most well-known locations.

Lahaina also provides a variety of traditional Hawaiian activities, like hula dance, lei making, and ukulele instruction, for visitors seeking a cultural experience. The conventional Hawaiian feast known as a luau, which features dance, music, and other cultural performances, is another option for tourists.

Lahaina is a must-see location for visitors to Maui due to its fascinating history, stunning beaches, and lively culture. You can find everything you're searching for in this little seaside town, whether you want to unwind, go on an adventure, or experience Hawaiian culture.

Beach at Kaanapali

On the western coast of Maui, Hawaii, there is a strikingly gorgeous and well-known beach called Kaanapali Beach. This three-mile stretch of golden sand is famous for its clear waters, excellent swimming conditions, and breathtaking sunsets, making it a popular destination for visitors and locals.

One of the top resort areas on the island, Kaanapali Beach is bordered by some of the best lodging options, dining establishments, and retail stores. Visitors can enjoy the breathtaking views of the Pacific Ocean, the adjacent islands of Lanai and Molokai, and the lush foliage of the West Maui Mountains by taking a stroll down the boardwalk that extends the length of the beach.

One of its highlights is the chance to snorkel or scuba dive in Kaanapali Beach's crystal-clear waters. A wide variety of marine life, including vibrant fish, sea turtles, and even manta rays, can be seen on the reef. For those who would rather stay on dry land, there is beach volleyball, swimming, and lounging in the sun on the sand.

Together with its scenic surroundings and fun activities, Kaanapali Beach is renowned for its cultural significance. Visitors can learn more about the area's history by going on a guided tour or going to the neighboring Whalers Village Museum. The beach was previously the location of a royal retreat.

In general, Kaanapali Beach is a must-visit location for tourists to Maui. It is an incredibly remarkable location that perfectly encapsulates Hawaii's island paradise due to its breathtaking beauty, a wide range of recreational options, and cultural significance.

Crater of Molokani

Off Maui, Hawaii's southern shore, sits the crescent-shaped island of Molokini Crater. It is a more than 400-foot-deep volcanic crater that rises roughly 160 feet above sea level and is only partially buried. Snorkelers and scuba divers from all over the world frequently travel to this distinctive and stunning geological structure.

With more than 250 species of fish and several kinds of coral, the Molokini Crater is home to a rich and varied marine ecology. Visitors may easily observe colorful schools of fish, marine turtles, and even the rare shark in the crystal-clear waters.

Tourists can take a guided snorkeling or scuba diving excursion to discover the underwater splendor of the crater. These excursions frequently include transportation to and from the hole, all required gear, and professional direction from experienced instructors. Swimming with dolphins and other marine creatures in the local waters is another feature of many cruises.

Molokini Crater has incredible natural beauty in addition to an intriguing past. A volcanic eruption created it over 230,000 years ago, and the U.S. Navy later used it as a target range during World War II. Some of Hawaii's most exquisite and vulnerable coral reefs can be found there, and it is now a protected marine sanctuary.

Molokini Crater is a favorite location for photographers due to its beautiful vistas of the island's rough shoreline and neighboring highlands and its recreational and educational activities.

In general, Molokini Crater is a must-visit location for tourists to Maui. Its unique location perfectly encapsulates Hawaii's natural beauty and cultural value due to its distinctive geological characteristics, diverse marine life, and rich history.

Park Iao Valley State

In the heart of Maui, Hawaii, there lies a stunning natural region called Iao Valley State Park. This verdant valley is renowned for its breathtaking mountain scenery, extensive past, and cultural value.

Visitors who want to take in the splendor of Hawaii's natural surroundings and discover the island's rich cultural history frequently travel there.

The Iao Needle, a massive rock formation towers over 1,200 feet above the valley floor, may be found in the park. The needle is a well-liked hiking destination with stunning views of the surroundings.

Visitors can explore the area's natural splendor up close on the park's numerous hiking paths, which snake through the thick greenery.

Iao Valley State Park is not only breathtakingly picturesque, but it is also incredibly significant historically and culturally. Nowadays, tourists can learn more about the region's history by visiting the Hawaii Nature Center or going on a guided tour with a local cultural expert.

The valley was once the scene of significant conflicts between competing Hawaiian chiefs. Several important religious sites are also located in the park, such as the Kepaniwai Park and Heritage Garden, which honor the cultural diversity of those who have made Hawaii home.

Iao Valley State Park is a well-liked vacation spot for history buffs, hikers, and environment lovers.

Tourists can enjoy the breathtaking valley vistas, hike through the verdant landscape, and discover the region's rich cultural history. It is an incredibly exceptional location that perfectly encapsulates Hawaii's natural beauty and cultural significance.

Ocean Center in Maui

The Maui Ocean Center aquarium is in Maalaea, Maui, Hawaii. This outstanding facility highlights the distinctive marine life in the Hawaiian Islands seas, providing visitors with a unique opportunity to interact closely with these fascinating creatures.

More than 60 displays, each representing a distinct component of Hawaii's marine ecosystem, may be found at the Maui Ocean Center. Guests can take in the splendor of vibrant tropical fish, get up and personal with majestic sea turtles, and discover more about the habits and habitats of sharks and other apex predators.

The center's main attraction is the Open Ocean exhibit, which includes a 750,000-gallon tank complete with various marine life, including rays, dolphins, and even sharks.

For guests of all ages, the center also provides a variety of educational and engaging experiences.

Visitors can participate in feeding sessions with some of the center's resident animals, experience a behind-the-scenes tour of the facilities, and listen to educational discussions and presentations by knowledgeable marine biologists.

The Maui Ocean Center is dedicated to marine conservation and research in addition to its exhibitions and educational offerings. The center is active in various research initiatives aimed at comprehending and conserving the area's delicate ecosystem and collaborates closely with local organizations to preserve Hawaii's maritime environment.

For anybody interested in the natural beauty and variety of Hawaii's marine life, the Maui Ocean Center is a must-visit location. It is a unique location that captures the essence of Hawaii's distinctive and priceless marine ecology with its top-notch exhibitions, educational offerings, and dedication to marine conservation.

Botanical Garden of Kula

On the mountainside of Haleakala, a dormant volcano on the Hawaiian island of Maui, is a stunning garden called Kula Botanical Garden. This 8-acre botanical garden contains a variety of plants from around the world, many of which are rare and endangered species.

The Botanical Garden was founded in 1970 by Warren and Helen McCord, who were passionate about horticulture and wanted to create a location where people could appreciate the beauty of nature. With more than 150,000 people annually, Kula Botanical Garden has expanded to become one of Maui's major tourist destinations.

The garden's collection of more than 2,500 plant species, which includes many exotic and tropical plants not found elsewhere on the island, is one of its standout characteristics. Tourists can take strolls through walkways adorned with vibrant flowers, tall trees, and bubbling streams while taking in the spectacular views of the mountains and ocean in the area.

Kula Botanical Garden is a well-liked location for visitors of all ages because it features a variety of other attractions in addition to its outstanding collection of plants.

There is a hummingbird habitat where guests may get up-close views of these little creatures and a waterfall and koi pond.

Qualified staff members offer guided tours for individuals who want to learn more about the plants and creatures in the garden. These tours provide a unique window into the garden's ecology and history and a chance to learn more about the many plant species and ask questions.

Therefore, everyone who enjoys the outdoors and wishes to witness the exquisiteness of Maui's flora and wildlife should notice Kula Botanical Garden. It is understandable why this garden has grown to be one of the island's most popular tourist destinations, given its breathtaking setting, varied plant collection, and educational opportunities.

Hawaii Bay

The Hawaiian island of Maui's northwest coast is home to the breathtakingly gorgeous bay known as Honolua Bay. The bay is renowned for its glistening seas, colorful coral reefs, and top-notch surf breaks. Snorkelers, divers, surfers, and environment enthusiasts from all over the world travel there frequently.

The Honolua-Mokuleia Bay Marine Life Conservation District, a protected region home to a staggering variety of marine species, is where the bay is located.

The bay is well-liked for snorkeling and diving since it has vibrant fish, sea turtles, and other marine life.

Along with having a rich undersea habitat, Honolua Bay is well known for having significant surf breaks. The Point and the Cave are the primary surfing locations in the bay. While the Cave is a shorter, more challenging wave better suited to advanced surfers, The Point is a long, right-hand break perfect for experienced surfers.

Honolua Bay is a well-liked location for natural strolls and hiking. Beautiful waterfalls, dense jungles, and expansive vistas of the Pacific Ocean may be found nearby. Visitors can experience the local natural beauty on one of the many hiking routes.

Honolua Bay should be noticed by everyone who enjoys the outdoors, nature, and adventure. It is one of the most popular locations in Hawaii and a true paradise for anyone who visits due to its crystal-clear waters, incredible surf breaks, and breathtaking natural beauty.

CHAPTER FOUR

Outdoor Activities in Maui

Outdoor lovers who want to explore nature and partake in various outdoor activities frequently travel to Maui, one of Hawaii's most stunning islands. The following are some of the best outdoor activities in Maui:

Scuba diving and snorkeling: The waters surrounding Maui are among the greatest in the world for these activities. Molokini Crater, Honolua Bay, and Black Rock are just a few locations where tourists can discover colorful coral reefs and varied aquatic life.

Surfing: World-class surfing locations on Maui include Honolua Bay, Ho'okipa Beach Park, and Peahi (also known as Jaws). Maui has waves for all kinds of surfers, whether you're a novice or an expert.

Hiking: Maui has many hiking paths, and they provide breathtaking views of the island's natural beauty. The Pipiwai Trail in Haleakala National Park, the Waihee Ridge Trail, and the Makawao Forest Reserve are all well-liked hiking routes.

Whale Watching: Maui is a great place to see whales from December to April. Tourists can join a boat trip to get a close-up look at the humpback whales.

Ziplining: The lush forests and valleys of Maui's island are traversed in an exhilarating journey by the island's several zipline courses. Ka'anapali and the Haleakala Crater are home to the most well-liked zipline courses.

Stand-up Paddleboarding: Visitors may explore the island's magnificent shoreline and tranquil waters by stand-up paddle boarding, a fun and peaceful pastime.

Kayaking: Tourists can use kayaks to explore Maui's crystal-clear waters and remote beaches. La Perouse Bay, Honolua Bay, and Makena Bay are well-liked kayaking locations.

Overall, Maui provides a variety of outdoor pursuits for adventurers of all skill levels. Maui offers thrilling and soothing experiences, so there's something for everyone.

CHAPTER FIVE

Best beaches in Maui

With white sand, clean oceans, and a spectacular landscape, Maui has some of the most beautiful beaches in the world. Some of Maui's top beaches are listed below:

Kaanapali Beach: One of the most well-liked beaches on the island is Kaanapali Beach, renowned for its golden sand and crystal-clear water. With several restaurants and businesses nearby, it's an excellent place for swimming, tanning, and snorkeling.

Wailea Beach: This beach is famed for its beautiful white sand and tranquil seas. It is situated in the luxury resort neighborhood of Wailea. Swimming, paddle boarding, and snorkeling are all excellent activities here, with gorgeous views of the adjacent islands.

Kapalua Bay Beach: is a gorgeous location for swimming, snorkeling, and sunbathing. This crescent-shaped beach is surrounded by lush flora and rocky outcroppings. It's a fantastic location for watching the sunset.

Makena Beach: often known as *"Big Beach,"* is one of Maui's most extended and stunning beaches. It is a long expanse of golden sand. There is plenty of room for everyone, making it a fantastic place for swimming and tanning.

Baldwin Beach: is a famous beach on Maui's north shore because of its extensive golden sand and sparkling water expanse. With several facilities nearby, it's an excellent place for swimming, surfing, and windsurfing.

Honolua Bay: With its beautiful water and abundant coral reefs, this scenic bay is well-liked for snorkeling and surfing. It's a terrific place to observe surfers catch some of the island's best waves and explore Maui's underwater ecology.

Family-friendly beaches

One of Hawaii's most visited islands, Maui, is renowned for its stunning beaches and crystal-clear waters, making it the perfect destination for families seeking an exciting beach getaway. The best beaches in Maui for families are listed below:

One of Maui's most well-known beaches, Kaanapali Beach has beautiful golden sand and tranquil waters that are ideal for swimming and snorkeling. A beach is a perfect place for families to spend the day because it is close to several hotels and dining establishments.

For those seeking a more private experience, Napili Beach is a fantastic family-friendly option. The beach provides opportunities for paddleboarding, snorkeling, calm waves, and lots of shade.

Another excellent family choice is Kapalua Beach, tucked away in a secluded cove where the seas are kept quiet and pristine. A beach is perfect for a family picnic because it has lots of shade and picnic tables.

A well-liked beach park with three distinct areas, Kamaole Beach Park is a terrific choice for families with children of all ages. The park is a practical choice for families because it offers lifeguards on duty, restrooms, showers, and enough parking.

Baby Beach is a fantastic choice for families with young children in Lahaina. The beach offers plenty of shelter, calm waves for swimming, and a shallow, safe section ideal for young children to play in.

Beaches with coral reefs

With its pristine seas and rich marine life, Maui, one of Hawaii's most visited islands, is a snorkeler's dream. Several stunning beaches on the island provide fantastic snorkeling opportunities. Here are a few of Maui's best snorkeling beaches:

Ka'anapali Beach: is a three-mile stretch of shoreline on Maui's west coast that is well-known for its snorkeling. Snorkelers can witness various marine life, including sea turtles, vibrant fish, and coral reefs, in the clear waters, providing excellent vision.

Napili Bay: Napili Bay is a protected cove with calm waters ideal for snorkeling. It is situated in West Maui. Various marine species, such as butterflyfish, parrotfish, and moray eels, call the reef home.

Honolua Bay: Because of its difficult circumstances, Honolua Bay on the northwest coast of Maui is a favorite location for experienced snorkelers. The protected bay is home to some of Maui's outstanding coral formations, which draw a variety of marine species.

Kapalua Bay: One of Maui's most scenic beaches, Kapalua Bay, has calm seas ideal for snorkeling. Many marine species, such as trumpetfish, surgeonfish, and damselfish, call the reef home.

Black Rock Beach is a well-known location for diving and snorkeling located at the northern end of Ka'anapali Beach. Many marine species, including sea turtles and vibrant fish, call the reef home.

Beaches with surfboards

With its crystal-clear waters, steady swells, and mild temperatures all year round, Maui is a surfer's paradise. In Maui, many beaches provide excellent surfing opportunities for novice and expert surfers.

Here are a few of Maui's top surfing beaches:

Honolua Bay is a well-known surf location for skilled surfers on Maui's northwest coast. The reef break produces excellent barrels; the waves can be up to 20 feet high.

Ho'okipa Beach: Ho'okipa Beach lies on Maui's north shore and is well-known for its dependable, strong surf. Moreover, kiteboarding and windsurfing are very popular there.

Lahaina Breakwall: is a well-known place for beginning and intermediate surfers on Maui's west coast. It's a fantastic area to learn how to surf because the waves are gentle to medium size, and the break is forgiving.

Kihei Cove: On Maui's south shore, Kihei Cove is a well-liked location for beginning surfers. The beach is relatively empty compared to other well-known surf locations on the island, and the waves are tiny and reliable.

Pe'ahi (Jaws): Pe'ahi, popularly known as Jaws, is one of the most well-known surf locations in the world and is situated on Maui's north shore. Only skilled surfers should attempt to ride the waves because they can be up to 60 feet high.

Launiupoko Beach Park: is a fantastic location for beginning and intermediate surfers on Maui's west coast. The beach is relatively empty compared to other well-liked surfing locations on the island, and the waves are tiny to medium-sized.

Beaches with no-clothing policies

Visitors can unwind on one of the stunning beaches on Maui, a gorgeous island in Hawaii while soaking up the sun and swimming in the crystal-clear seas.

There are beaches on Maui where tourists can enjoy the freedom of going nude if they want a distinctive experience.

At Makena State Park, Little Beach is a well-liked beach in Maui where visitors are not required to cover up. This remote beach's stunning blue seas and fine white sand are well recognized. It's a beautiful location for swimming and enjoying the sunshine without any wardrobe restrictions.

Red Sand Beach, also known as Kaihalulu Beach, is another beach in Maui where you are not required to cover up. This beach is in Hana and is well-known for its distinctive red sand. Guests can enjoy the seclusion of this beach and the ability to go nude while taking in the breathtaking surroundings.

If you're looking for a beach in Maui where you can go without clothes, another choice is Polo Beach. This

South Maui beach is well-known for its crystal-clear waters and excellent snorkeling. Tourists can swim naked while observing the vibrant fish and sea turtles swimming past.

Although clothing-optional beaches are permitted on Maui, it's vital to remember that tourists should also show consideration for those who might not find nudity to their taste. Additionally, because these beaches are frequently inaccessible and may need amenities like restrooms or showers, it's crucial to bring sunscreen, water, and other necessary beach equipment.

In conclusion, for those looking to enjoy the freedom of going naked while soaking up the sun and taking in the island's natural beauty, Maui's clothing-optional beaches provide a unique and wonderful experience.

CHAPTER SIX

Traditional Hawaiian cuisine

Hawaiian culture and history are only complete with traditional cuisine. Hawaii's cuisine reflects the island's distinct geography, climate, and cultural influences. Fresh fish, taro, sweet potatoes, coconut, and other tropical fruits are staples of traditional Hawaiian cuisine.

Poke, a dish made with cubed raw fish and often marinated in soy sauce, sesame oil, and other seasonings, is one of the most well-known dishes of Hawaiian cuisine. Poke can be eaten by itself or as part of a poke bowl with rice.

Another notable Hawaiian meal is **"kalua pig,"** which is slow-roasted pork prepared in an "imu," an underground oven. Before being cooked in the imu, the meat is seasoned with sea salt and wrapped in ti leaves.

Traditional Hawaiian food includes **taro**, frequently used to make "poi," a mashed, purple-colored paste popular in Hawaii. Taro is a crucial ingredient in this dish. Taro is steamed or baked, then mashed with water to a smooth, pudding-like consistency to make poi.

Laulau is a different classic Hawaiian food prepared by wrapping pork, poultry, or fish in taro leaves and cooking it in an imu. The ultimate product is a soft, savory dish, frequently served with rice and poi.

A significant component in Hawaiian cooking is coconut, used to make meals like "haupia," a pudding made with coconut milk frequently given as a dessert. Salted foods like "chicken long rice," a soup with chicken, ginger, and garlic cooked in coconut milk, also contain coconut.

Hawaii has been influenced by the cuisines of other cultures, including Japanese, Chinese, Filipino, and Portuguese, in addition to these traditional delicacies.

As a result, extraordinary fusion foods like "spam musubi," a snack similar to sushi made with grilled Spam and rice, and "plate lunch," a meal often made out of rice, macaroni salad, and a meat dish like teriyaki chicken or kalbi ribs, have been produced.

Maui's top restaurants

Maui is a magnificent island in Hawaii, well-known for its gorgeous beaches, verdant landscape, and mouthwatering cuisine.

Many restaurants on the island serve food from all over the world as well as traditional Hawaiian cooking. These are a few of the top dining establishments in Maui that you ought to visit:

One of Maui's most well-known eateries is Mama's Fish House on the North Shore. It has a large selection of dishes made with fresh seafood, and the ambiance is casual and welcoming.

The award-winning Lahaina eatery **Lahaina Grill** is well-known for its modern American fare. The menu offers creative meals such as the Kona Lobster and Crab Cake and Ahi Tuna Nachos, made using locally sourced ingredients.

Farm-to-table dining is served at Merriman's Maui in Kapalua, focusing on Hawaiian products. The menu offers meals like the Local Island Taro, Vegetable Lasagna, Kauai Shrimp, and Pork Belly.

The **Mill House in Waikapu** provides a distinctive dining experience focusing on sustainability. The restaurant is located on a functioning plantation, and the menu includes meals produced with regional products.

Oceanfront eatery Leilani's On The Beach in Kaanapali is well-known for its breathtaking vistas and delectable seafood fare. The menu offers traditional dishes, including Lobster, Crab Bisque, and Fish & Chips.

A trip **to Kihei's Koiso Sushi Bar** is essential for sushi fans. Traditional sushi and sashimi dishes are on the menu, and chef-owner Hiro-san is renowned for his skill and attention to detail.

Various noodle meals and small plates are available at Lahaina's Star Noodle, an Asian-inspired eatery. The Hapa Ramen and the Pork Belly Bao are just a few items on the menu.

Overall, Maui has some of Hawaii's top dining establishments. There is food on the island for everyone, whether you're in the mood for inventive cuisine or fresh fish.

Breweries and distilleries in the area

Hawaii's island of Maui is renowned for its gorgeous beaches, spectacular scenery, and delectable cuisine. The island has recently developed into a center for neighborhood breweries and distilleries, with several of these businesses making craft beer and spirits from local ingredients. Here are a few of Maui's best craft brewers and distilleries:

Brewing Company of Maui: One of the biggest and most well-known brewers on the island is The Maui Brewing Company. The company, founded in 2005, makes a variety of beers, including the well-known Bikini Blonde Lager and Big Swell IPA.

Visitors can try the brews and eat delectable food at the brewery's restaurant and tasting area.

Kohola Brewery: is a family-run brewery in Lahaina specializing in making small-batch craft brews. The native flavors and customs of Hawaii serve as inspiration for the brewery's beers, which are brewed with locally obtained ingredients. The Red Sand Ale and Pineapple Lokahi Pilsner are the brewery's most well-liked brews.

Hali'imaile Distilling Company: This neighborhood distillery creates a variety of acclaimed spirits, including vodka, rum, and whiskey. The distillery in upcountry Maui offers tours and tastings where guests may discover the distilling procedure and partake in some delectable spirits.

Ocean Vodka: Using organic sugar cane and deep ocean mineral water from Hawaii, Ocean Vodka is a family-run distillery that creates vodka. Kula is home to the distillery's tasting room, which boasts spectacular ocean and island views.

Even though it's neither a brewery nor a distillery, Maui Wine is a must-go for everyone interested in trying locally-made libations. The winery creates a variety of acclaimed wines, including its well-known pineapple wine, which is designed with pineapples produced in Maui.

Overall, Maui's indigenous distilleries and breweries give tourists a distinctive and delectable way to explore the island's culture.

The local breweries and distilleries on Maui have something for everyone, whether you enjoy beer or spirits or want to experience something new.

Farmers' markets and food trucks

With abundant locally grown fresh vegetables, seafood, and a combination of international culinary influences, Maui is renowned for its thriving food scene. The island's farmer's markets and food trucks are well-liked ways to sample its culinary scene.

Food trucks: A mainstay of Maui's culinary scene, food trucks provide both locals and visitors with a broad selection of delectable and reasonably priced meals. Maui's food trucks give various cuisines, from local specialties to international fare. On the island, some of the most well-known food trucks are:

Garlic shrimp, served with a side of rice and maize, are the specialty of the Geste Shrimp food truck.

Pad thai and sticky mango rice are just some Thai and Hawaiian-inspired dishes available at Aloha Thai Fusion.

Three's Bar and Grill Food Truck has something for everyone, from burgers and tacos to poke bowls and salads.

Hornitos Mobile Taqueria: This well-known food truck offers mouthwatering tacos and burritos with various filling choices.

Shark Pit Maui: should be on your travel itinerary if you enjoy seafood. This food truck offers ceviche, poke bowls and fresh fish tacos.

Farmer's markets: Maui has many farmer's markets where tourists can sample locally produced foods and handcrafted goods. On the island, some of the busiest farmer's markets are:

The Maui Swap Meet is a weekly market in Kahului that sells various native goods, including fresh produce, handcrafted items, and clothes.

Every Saturday, the Upcountry Farmer's Market in Kula offers a selection of locally produced foods such as avocados, tomatoes, and citrus fruits.

Lahaina Farmer's Market: This market, held every Thursday in Lahaina, sells a variety of handcrafted crafts, baked goods, and fresh produce.

Every Wednesday, the Napili Farmer's Market offers a range of locally grown fruits and vegetables and handcrafted goods, including jewelry and crafts.

At Kula Country Farms, guests can buy fresh fruit, jams, and baked products at a farmer's market in addition to the farm's well-known pumpkin patch in the fall.

Overall, visiting food trucks and farmer's markets is a fantastic opportunity to see Maui's diverse culinary scene and help out the local economy. Maui's food trucks and farmer's markets have something for everyone, whether you're searching for a quick and delicious lunch on the go or want to sample some fresh, locally grown veggies.

CHAPTER SEVEN

Bars and clubs in Maui

Maui offers something for everyone, whether you want to relax with friends, dance the night away to live music or sip on a tropical beverage while admiring the ocean.

Nightlife in Maui

Lahaina, a historic town on Maui's west coast, is one of the most well-liked spots for nightlife. Many bars and clubs that accommodate all tastes and preferences can be found here.

For instance, rock icon Mick Fleetwood owns the upscale rooftop bar and restaurant Fleetwood's on Front St., with live music performances and breathtaking ocean views. In contrast, Down the Hatch is a more relaxed pub and eatery with a wide variety of craft beers and delectable tapas.

If you're searching for a club scene, Kihei, a seaside town on Maui, is the place to go. There are places like The Dirty Monkey, renowned for its energetic ambiance and well-known DJs spinning dance music. Mulligans on the Blue, a bar and restaurant featuring live music performances that include reggae, rock, and blues, is another well-liked destination in Kihei.

Other notable bars and clubs in Maui include Charley's Restaurant and Saloon in Paia, a storied establishment hosting well-known musicians like Willie Nelson and Mick Fleetwood over the years Monkeypod Kitchen in Wailea, which features a laid-back atmosphere and an impressive selection of craft cocktails.

The legal drinking age in Hawaii is 21, and entry to most pubs and clubs in Maui requires a valid ID. Also, organizing a designated driver or alternate transportation is a good idea if you intend to drink.

Nevertheless, Maui has a thriving nighttime culture with various options to accommodate different tastes and budgets. In Maui's pubs and clubs, you may find anything from a calm evening with a tropical cocktail to a wild night of dancing and partying.

Concert venues

Live music lovers frequently go to Maui, where various venues feature local and foreign talent. You're sure to find a performance that appeals to your tastes, whether you're in the mood for rock, jazz, reggae, or traditional Hawaiian music.

The Maui Arts and Cultural Center, situated in Kahului, is one of Maui's most recognizable locations for live music. This cutting-edge venue presents a range of concerts and performances throughout the year that feature regional and world-famous performers. The platform serves a variety of musical genres and has numerous stages, including an outdoor amphitheater and a smaller interior theater.

Look inside **Wailuku's old Iao Theater** for a more secluded environment. This exquisitely restored theater, built in 1928, presents a range of entertainment, including plays, musicals, and concerts. The theater is a fantastic location to enjoy live music in a distinctive, historic setting with a long history.

Visit **Charley's Restaurant and Bar in Paia** for a more relaxed ambiance. Over the years, this storied venue has welcomed well-known musicians like Willie Nelson and Mick Fleetwood and has hosted live music concerts for over 50 years. The facility provides a variety of musical styles, including rock, reggae, and Hawaiian music, and presents live performances virtually every night of the week.

Casanova in Makawao is yet another fantastic choice for live music in Maui. This event attracts residents and tourists since it has a mix of touring performers and a lively environment.

The location boasts a full bar and restaurant, making it a perfect place to enjoy live music and delectable food for the evening.

Mulligans on the Blue in Kihei, which presents live music seven nights a week and features a variety of genres, including jazz and blues, and the Maui Coffee Attic in Wailuku, which regularly organizes open mic nights and highlights local talent, are two more famous live music venues in Maui.

Cultural festivals and luaus

Hawaii's cultural and historical center is Maui, which has a strong history in storytelling, music, and dance.

Attending a luau or cultural event is one of the most significant ways to experience the local culture since you may take in Hawaiian history and customs while enjoying traditional cuisine, music, and entertainment.

The Old Lahaina Luau, situated in Lahaina, is one of the most well-known luaus on Maui. Traditional Hawaiian cuisine, live Hawaiian music, and hula shows are all included in this award-winning luau's real Hawaiian experience.

Visitors may learn about Hawaii's history and culture through hands-on activities and storytelling at the event, which is held in a lovely beachside location.

The **Feast at Lele** in Lahaina is another well-known luau. With a gourmet five-course lunch inspired by Polynesian cuisine and live performances featuring the music and dance of Hawaii, Tahiti, Samoa, and New Zealand, this luxury event delivers a more personal and abundant experience.

The Bailey House Museum in Wailuku provides a variety of cultural activities and exhibitions for anyone interested in learning more about Hawaiian history and culture. The museum exhibits Hawaiian antiquities, like costumes, weaponry, and tools, and also provides workshops and instructional programs on Hawaiian crafts and traditions.

The Maui County Fair held yearly at Wailuku is a cultural event that should be noticed. The fair features a variety of entertainment options, such as carnival games, carnival rides, and live performances by regional dancers and singers. Visitors can enjoy some traditional Hawaiian cuisine by learning about Maui and Hawaii's history and culture.

Last but not least, Kahului hosts the annual Maui Matsuri festival, which celebrates Japanese culture and traditions. Among the events available at the festival are taiko drum performances, martial arts exhibitions, and traditional Japanese cuisine and crafts.

CHAPTER EIGHT

Shopping in Maui

Beautiful Maui in Hawaii is renowned for its magnificent beaches, verdant forests, and lively culture. Visits to the different local markets and boutiques that can be found all around the island are one of the finest ways to learn about the culture and support the local economy.

Local markets and boutiques

The Maui Swap Meet, which takes place every Saturday at the University of Hawaii Maui College, is one well-liked neighborhood market in Maui.

Here, guests may browse through more than 200 vendors selling everything from clothing and trinkets to locally crafted crafts and fresh fruit. Visitors are sure to love the lively atmosphere and hospitable locals at the market, which is a terrific place to find distinctive and authentic goods.

The **Upcountry Farmers Market,** which is held in the town of Kula every Saturday morning, is another fantastic market to check out while visiting Maui. In addition to a wide selection of artisanal goods including honey, baked goods, and handcrafted items, this market is widely renowned for its fresh produce, which includes locally grown fruits and vegetables.

Maui is also home to a handful of boutique stores that provide a distinctive shopping experience in addition to these marketplaces.

In the town of Paia, **Pearl Butik** is one well-known store. At this store, you'll find a carefully curated collection of accessories, jewelry, and clothes for women made by regional designers. Wings Hawaii is another fantastic store to check out; it has a wide selection of apparel and accessories that are motivated by the natural beauty of the island.

Overall, shopping in Maui's local markets and boutiques is a terrific opportunity to support the community's economy and experience the island's distinctive culture. From fresh fruit and handcrafted crafts to locally made clothing and accessories, there is something for everyone to enjoy.

Gifts and mementos

Hawaii's Maui is a well-liked holiday spot because of its breathtaking beaches, picturesque surroundings, and lively culture. As a means to remember their journey and share their experience with loved ones back home, many tourists to Maui take pleasure in bringing gifts and mementos home.

Here are some well-liked gifts and mementos to take into account when visiting Maui:

Hawaiian shirts and dresses: are a traditional Hawaii souvenir, and Maui has no shortage of stores that sell them. These vibrant outfits are ideal for wearing on a tropical vacation or as a fun and festive look for special occasions. They contain typical Hawaiian themes like hibiscus flowers, palm palms, and ocean waves.

Handcrafted Jewelry: The island of Maui is home to many creative jewelers who craft one-of-a-kind, exquisite items from the island's shells, coral, and semi-precious stones. You're sure to find something special to bring home as a memento, whether you're looking for a bold necklace, a delicate bracelet, or a pair of earrings.

Local Art: Maui is home to a bustling art industry with a number of galleries and studios showing the creations of local artists. There are numerous possibilities for art enthusiasts wishing to carry a piece of Maui's creative energy home, ranging from paintings and sculptures to ceramics and glasswork.

Food and Drink: Maui's food is just as delectable as the rest of Hawaii's. With goodies like macadamia nuts, Kona coffee, Maui-made chocolate, and local jams and honey, tourists can bring a taste of the island home. Also, you can buy a bottle of regional craft beer or wine to enjoy at home.

Hawaiian quilts are a distinctive and exquisite memento of Maui. These handcrafted quilts were created utilizing the "applique" technique, in which fabric shapes are sewn onto a background cloth to form a design. The quilts' typical Hawaiian patterns include flowers and tropical birds. Hawaiian quilts are a lovely and helpful memento ideal for cuddling up on the sofa or displaying as a work of art.

Ukuleles: The ukulele is a traditional Hawaiian instrument, and Maui is home to several stores that focus on selling and repairing ukuleles. A ukulele from Maui is a terrific option whether you're a musician or just looking for a fun and distinctive memento.

Attractive stores in Wailea

On the Hawaiian island of Maui, there is a lovely resort area called Wailea that is well-known for its magnificent beaches, fine dining establishments, and premium retail stores. Visitors and residents enjoy luxury shopping in Wailea, which has a wide selection of boutiques and designer stores that sell everything from apparel and jewelry to home goods and fine art.

The Shops at Wailea, a beautifully manicured outdoor retail mall with over 70 businesses and restaurants, is one of Wailea's most well-liked shopping areas. Designer labels like Gucci, Prada, and Louis Vuitton and upscale stores like Tiffany & Co. and Neiman Marcus are available here.

Many regional boutiques and specialized stores may be found in The Shops at Wailea, selling everything from artisanal foods to home furnishings and handmade jewelry. There are several other upscale stores in the region besides The Shops at Wailea. Several upscale businesses providing apparel, accessories, and home furnishings are housed at the on-site shopping center of the Grand Wailea Resort.

Another exclusive resort in Wailea, the Fairmont Kea Lani, has its shopping area with shops selling anything from designer swimwear to locally made pottery and artwork.

There are several local artists and galleries in Wailea if you want something unique. Several of these artists produce unique paintings, sculptures, and jewelry inspired by the island's natural beauty.

Visits to these galleries are essential for art lovers and collectors since they offer the chance to see and purchase original works of art that cannot be found anywhere else in the world.

CHAPTER NINE

Wellness and Spa in Maui - Yoga and meditation

Yoga and meditation are best practiced in Wailea, a stunning seaside resort area on the Hawaiian island of Maui. Worldwide, yoga and meditation have gained popularity as forms of fitness and relaxation. Wailea provides a calm and quiet setting for people looking to develop a closer relationship with their inner selves.

Yoga is a type of exercise that focuses on breath and mindfulness while stretching, strengthening, and balancing the body. In Wailea, there are a lot of yoga studios that provide instruction for all skill levels, from beginning to advanced.

Several studios even deliver outdoor courses to lush tropical gardens or on the beach, which offers a relaxing and immersing environment.

Deep breathing exercises are frequently done with meditation, a technique for focusing on the present moment and quieting the mind. It has been demonstrated that meditation improves general mental and emotional well-being by lowering stress, anxiety, and depression. There are numerous options to meditate in Wailea, ranging from led group programs to solitary practice in serene outdoor settings.

As a part of their wellness initiatives, several Wailea resorts and retreat facilities now provide yoga and meditation courses. Some even offer retreats incorporating yoga, meditation, and other wellness techniques like massage, acupuncture, and nutritious food.

The serene and peaceful atmosphere of Wailea's natural beauty makes for the ideal setting for yoga and meditation practice. The sound of the ocean waves, the palm palms' rustle, and the tropical flowers' aroma all contribute to the area's tranquility. Wailea provides a variety of chances for you to develop your practice and connect with your inner self, whether you are an experienced practitioner or a beginning.

Massages and spa services

On Maui, Hawaii's southern coast is the lovely resort community of Wailea. It is renowned for its magnificent beaches, opulent hotels, and top-notch spas. You won't be disappointed if you seek a stimulating and refreshing spa experience in Wailea. Here are a few top spa services and massages available in Wailea.

Hawaiian Lomi Lomi Massage: This traditional Hawaiian massage aims to calm the body and unwind the mind. It uses sweeping, flowing strokes meant to resemble the motion of the water. The massage therapist applies deep tissue pressure with their hands, forearms, and elbows to relieve tension and boost circulation. Also, the Lomi Lomi massage has a reputation for fostering well-being, balance, and healing.

Hot Stone Massage: Wailea offers many popular spa services, including hot stone massage. With this massage, heated basalt stones are applied to the body at strategic locations.

The heat from the rocks aids in easing tension and relaxing the muscles. The massage therapist also employs stones for deep tissue massage to treat pain and stiffness in the muscles.

Hawaiian Salt Scrub: Using sea salt, coconut oil, and essential oils to exfoliate the skin, the Hawaiian Salt Scrub is a well-liked spa treatment in Wailea.

Dead skin cells will be removed throughout this procedure, leaving the skin feeling smooth and soft. The Hawaiian Salt Scrub also aids in relaxation and stress reduction.

Aromatherapy Massage: A relaxing massage technique that uses essential oils to encourage calm and lessen tension is known as aromatherapy massage.

The oils are applied to the skin, and their scent is released by the massage therapist using various techniques. The essential oils, including lavender, peppermint, eucalyptus, and many more, are chosen for their medicinal effects.

Facial Treatments: Another well-liked spa service in Wailea is facial treatments. They are made to moisturize, exfoliate, and clean the skin. The Hydrating Facial, Anti-Aging Facial, and Oxygen Facial are some of the most popular facial treatments.

These procedures use several methods, including steam, masks, and serums, to enhance the skin's appearance and leave it feeling rejuvenated.

Wailea is an excellent choice for anyone seeking a tranquil and revitalizing spa experience. You are guaranteed to find the ideal spa service to help you relax and recharge with the variety of spa services and massages available.

Outdoor exercises for health

The "Valley Isle" of Maui is one of the most stunning and serene places on earth. The island is ideal for outdoor wellness activities because of its clean beaches, rich tropical rainforests, and majestic mountains. Here are some things to do to refresh and unwind while admiring Maui's natural beauty.

Hiking: Maui offers a variety of gorgeous hikes, from simple to complex. With trails leading to beautiful waterfalls and expansive island vistas, the Haleakala National Park is a fantastic area to explore. The Pipiwai Trail in the island's east leads to the breathtaking Waimoku Waterfall after passing through a bamboo grove.

Yoga: Maui's stunning natural surroundings make it the ideal location to practice yoga. You can connect with nature and discover inner serenity by taking a yoga class on the beach, which several studios offer. On the island, there are yoga retreats and workshops where you can hone your skills and meet others who share your interests.

Surfing: There is no better way to connect with the ocean than by riding its waves, and Maui is known for having world-class surfing locations. Beginner surfing lessons are available, while seasoned surfers can test their skills at locations including Honolua Bay and Peahi (also known as Jaws).

Snorkeling: The world's most stunning coral reefs may be found in Maui, and snorkeling is the best way to see them. Molokini Crater is a well-liked destination with its pristine waters and much marine life, including colorful fish, sea turtles, and even reef sharks.

Stand-Up Paddle boarding: Stand-up paddleboarding (SUP) is a fun and effective way to explore Maui's shoreline. Several beaches offer SUP rentals, and you can go on guided tours that take you through tranquil lagoons and mangrove woods.

Whale watching: Humpback whales migrate to Maui's warm waters from December to April to breed and give birth. You may take whale-watching cruises to see these magnificent animals up close.

CHAPTER TEN

Best family-friendly attractions

For families seeking a tropical vacation, Maui is a great choice. The island provides a range of experiences with its gorgeous beaches, lush jungles, and thrilling attractions that will keep everyone entertained. Some of Maui's top family-friendly attractions are listed below:

The Maui Ocean Center is a top-notch aquarium that highlights the distinctive marine life of Hawaii. In addition to a touch pool and a 750,000-gallon tank with sharks, rays, and other marine life, the center has interactive exhibits.

Families should visit Haleakala National Park, which is a must-see location. The park's hiking routes are appropriate for hikers of all ages and experience levels, and it offers beautiful views of Maui's volcanic environment. The park is also home to the state bird of Hawaii, the critically endangered nene goose.

Road to Hana: The Road to Hana is a beautiful journey that travels along Maui's breathtaking coastline and lush jungles. Along the way, you'll pass by waterfalls, beaches, and other family-friendly sites.

A thriving farm that provides guided tours through its fields of tropical fruits and flowers is called the Maui Tropical Plantation. A zipline course, a train ride, and a restaurant serving farm-to-table fare are also available at the plantation.

Lahaina Town: Once a whaling community, Lahaina Town today houses a variety of stores, eateries, and galleries. The town also has some museums, including the Whalers Village Museum and the Baldwin House Museum.

The Sugar Cane Railway: is a vintage railroad that offers scenic rides through the sugar cane fields of Maui. The railway has open-air coaches, so you can enjoy the island's beauty and learn about its fascinating history.

Finally, Maui has many family-friendly attractions that will keep everyone entertained. The island has much to offer everyone, whether they like snorkeling at the Maui Ocean Center or taking a picturesque drive to Hana.

Family-friendly beaches

Many of Maui's stunning beaches are ideal for families with young children. These beaches provide kids of all ages with various activities, calm waves, and soft sand. Here are some of Maui's top family-friendly beaches:

Kaanapali Beach: Kaanapali Beach is one of Maui's most popular beaches and offers a wide range of family activities. The beach is perfect for swimming, snorkeling, and stand-up paddle boarding, and several restaurants and shops are nearby.

Kamaole Beach Park: Kamaole Beach Park is a series of three beaches that offer calm waters and soft sand. The park features picnic areas, playgrounds, and restrooms, making it ideal for families with children.

Napili Bay: Napili Bay is a quiet beach perfect for families with young children. The beach offers calm waters and a protected cove, making it an excellent spot for swimming and snorkeling. There are also several restaurants and shops nearby.

Baby Beach: Baby Beach is a small, shallow beach perfect for toddlers and young children. The beach offers calm waters and a protected cove, making it an ideal spot for young swimmers.

Kapalua Beach: Kapalua Beach is a beautiful, secluded beach perfect for families. The beach offers calm waters, soft sand, and several shaded areas where families can relax and enjoy the view.

Charley Young Beach: Charley Young Beach is a small, quiet beach perfect for families with young children. The beach offers calm waters and a protected cove, making it an excellent spot for swimming and snorkeling.

Activities for kids and teens

Maui is a paradise for kids and teens. So many exciting activities on the island will keep children of all ages entertained. From exploring the island's natural wonders to trying out new sports and activities, Maui has something for everyone.

Here are some of the best exercises for kids and teens in Maui:

Snorkeling: Maui has some of the best snorkeling spots in the world, and it's an excellent activity for kids and teens. Children as young as five can try snorkeling, and plenty of tours and rentals are available on the island.

Surfing: Surfing is a quintessential Maui activity, and plenty of surf schools on the island cater to kids and teens. Surf lessons are available for children as young as five, and there are plenty of beginner-friendly spots to try.

Ziplining. Kids and teenagers will enjoy the thrilling pastime of ziplining. Throughout the island, there are several zipline courses, some of which provide breathtaking vistas of Maui's natural splendor.

Hiking: Maui is home to several fantastic hiking routes appropriate for children and teenagers. For instance, the Waihee Ridge Trail suits older kids and teenagers and gives breathtaking island views.

Whale watching: Humpback whales live in Maui's seas from December to May. Kids and teenagers will adore a whale-watching excursion, which is a fantastic experience.

Maui features several aquariums and museums that are ideal for children and teenagers. For instance, the Sugar Museum provides a fascinating look at the island's sugar business, while the Maui Ocean Center is a top-notch aquarium that displays Hawaii's distinctive marine life.

In conclusion, Maui has a variety of kid and teen-friendly activities that will keep them occupied and entertained. There is something for everyone on this lovely island, whether they choose to explore the island's natural treasures or try out novel sports and activities.

CHAPTER ELEVEN

LGBTQ+ Maui - LGBTQ+ friendly activities and events

Hawaii's Maui Island is a stunning multicultural location with a vibrant LGBTQ+ community. Throughout the island, there are many LGBTQ+-friendly activities and events to participate in. Some of the best choices are as follows:

Every year, the LGBTQ+ community on the island of Maui is honored at the Maui Pride Festival. The celebration includes a procession, live music, food, and goods vendors. It's a fantastic way to meet people in the neighborhood and voice your support for LGBTQ+ rights.

Beaches: Visitors identifying as LGBTQ+ are welcome at Maui's many stunning beaches. The LGBTQ+ community enjoys Little Beach because it is a beach where clothes are not required. LGBTQ+-

friendly beaches may be found in Ho'okipa Beach Park and Baldwin Beach Park, among others.

Scuba diving and snorkeling: Maui has some of the world's top locations for these sports. There are many possibilities for experiencing the undersea environment, regardless of your level of diving expertise. Honolua Bay and Molokini Crater are two popular locations.

Hiking: The lovely hiking paths on Maui provide breathtaking island views. The Pipiwai Trail, Waihee Ridge Trail, and Haleakala Crater Trek are well-liked possibilities. Just remember to pack plenty of water and sun protection!

The Maui Film Festival is an annual occasion where independent movies worldwide are shown. Screenings, panel discussions, and parties are all part of the festival in June. It's a beautiful way to take in some culture and support LGBTQ+ creators.

In general, LGBTQ+ guests will find Maui a friendly and accepting destination. There are many activities and events to choose from, whether you want to meet people in the neighborhood or take in some of the island's natural beauty.

Gay clubs and bars

Although Maui is not known for having a vibrant nightlife, travelers who identify as LGBTQ+ still have a few options for a night out. On the island, you can find the following gay bars and clubs:

Playbar Maui is a well-known gay bar that is situated in Kihei. It's a relaxed setting where you can drink and talk to people from the neighborhood and other visiting people. They also have a jukebox, a pool table, and occasionally live music.

Diamonds Ice Bar and Grill: Located in Kihei, Diamonds Ice Bar and Grill is a restaurant and bar that provides a fun environment and a range of entertainment alternatives. Every Tuesday, they offer a karaoke night; other nights, there are drag acts and live music. The diamonds Ice bar and Grill is where you should go to have an excellent time in the city.

Ambrosia Martini Lounge: This hip restaurant and bar in Kihei offers mouthwatering cocktails and light fare. Both locals and visitors enjoy going there, and there are frequent events like quiz nights and live music.

Pau Vodka Bar: is a little place in Lahaina that specializes in artisan drinks made with locally found ingredients. They occasionally have live music and a small dance floor, so it's a beautiful location to hang out with friends. While there aren't many specifically gay bars and clubs on Maui, those that do offer a warm and friendly environment for LGBTQ+ guests eager to experience the island's nightlife.

LGBTQ+-friendly facilities

The second-largest Hawaiian island, Maui, is renowned for its breathtaking beaches, unspoiled natural beauty, and friendly, inviting vibe. It's good to know that there are many LGBTQ+-friendly lodging options on Maui if you're a member of the LGBTQ+ community planning a trip there. Here are a few possibilities:

Located in Kihei, **the Maui Sunseeker LGBT Resort** is open only to visitors who identify as LGBTQ+. It provides cozy rooms and suites, a hot tub, and an attire-optional pool. The hotel also features a rooftop deck with breathtaking ocean views, where LGBTQ+ parties and activities are frequently held.

Andaz Maui at Wailea Resort: This opulent Wailea resort is renowned for its breathtaking oceanfront setting, roomy accommodations, and first-rate amenities. The staff is famous for being hospitable and sympathetic to LGBTQ+ visitors.

Hotel Wailea: This Wailea hotel for adults only is renowned for its seclusion and exclusivity. The hotel has breathtaking ocean views and is tucked away in a lush tropical environment. LGBTQ+ visitors are known to be welcomed and accepted by the personnel.

Kohea Kai Maui: is a boutique hotel in Kihei that is renowned for its superb position just feet from the beach and its contemporary, comfortable suites. The hotel boasts a welcoming, inclusive atmosphere and is receptive to LGBTQ+ guests.

Fairmont Kea Lani: This opulent Wailea resort is renowned for its roomy accommodations, first-rate amenities, and breathtaking ocean views.

The resort often sponsors LGBTQ+ events and activities, and the staff is famous for being hospitable and accepting to LGBTQ+ visitors.

Here are just a few of Maui lodgings that welcome LGBTQ+ travelers. You can anticipate a cheerful, welcoming ambiance and a warm welcome anywhere you stay on the island.

CHAPTER TWELVE.

Sustainable Tourism in Maui - Ecotourism in Maui

Ecotourism has grown in appeal on the island due to a commitment to sustainability and the preservation of its natural resources.

Visitors may explore and appreciate the island's nature while having as little of an impact as possible on the fragile ecosystems thanks to ecotourism. Rich rainforests, rocky coasts, and brilliant coral reefs are just a few of Maui's distinctive and varied ecosystems.

Many ecotourism activities, including hiking, snorkeling, and whale viewing, are available to visitors. Visitors can participate in these activities while learning about the island's distinctive ecosystems and how crucial it is to preserve them.

Hiking is a well-liked ecotourism activity in Maui. Visitors can explore the island's rainforests, waterfalls, and volcanic vistas by hiking on one of the island's many routes, ranging from easy to complex.

The Haleakala Crater climb, which leads visitors through a volcanic crater and offers breathtaking island views, is among the most well-liked hikes.

Snorkeling is another well-liked ecotourism activity in Maui. Sea turtles, vibrant fish, and even whales can be found in plenty of the island's coral reefs. Guests can participate in narrated snorkeling excursions that educate them on the value of preserving reefs and the marine species that live inside them.

Another well-liked ecotourism activity on Maui is whale viewing. Humpback whales migrate to the island's warm waters from December to May, where they mate and give birth.

The opportunity to view these magnificent creatures up close while learning about their habits and conservation efforts is provided by guided whale-watching trips available to tourists.

As a result of the dedication of numerous hotels and restaurants to sustainability and minimizing their adverse environmental effects, Maui also provides eco-friendly lodging and dining options.

Guests have various eco-friendly lodging options, including eco-lodges made of sustainable materials and hotels that use renewable energy.

Finally, Maui's ecotourism allows travelers to see and discover the island's natural beauty while discovering the significance of preservation and sustainability. Maui is an excellent place for anyone looking for an eco-friendly holiday because of its dedication to protecting its natural resources.

Responsible travel practices

One of Hawaii's most well-liked vacation spots is Maui, renowned for its stunning beaches, picturesque scenery, and diverse cultural heritage.

Appropriate travel habits must be adopted to safeguard the sustainability of the island and maintain its natural beauty for future generations. Tourism does, however, come with responsibilities.

While visiting Maui, be sure to adhere to the following responsible travel guidelines:

Respect the Culture: Maui has a vibrant cultural history. Therefore it's crucial to keep in mind and respect the local ways of life. Whether visiting holy places, attending rituals, or participating in cultural activities, be aware of your behavior, educate yourself about the local culture, and dress appropriately.

Support local businesses, farmers, and craftspeople when you visit Maui. Dine at neighborhood eateries, get souvenirs from neighborhood stores, and participate in neighborhood businesses' tours and activities. This will contribute to the sustainability of the **neighborhood** and the local economy.

Bring your reusable water bottle to restaurants or water fountains to reduce waste. Avoid using single-use plastics like straws, bags, and utensils, and use sustainable substitutes instead. Recycle whenever you can and dispose of your garbage responsibly.

Beaches in Maui are popular tourist destinations but are also delicate ecosystems. Don't walk on the dunes or the vegetation along the coast, and don't destroy or harm any coral or marine life. Leave only your tracks behind and abide by all beach rules.

Select Eco-Friendly Hotels or Resorts: When making your reservations, look for eco-friendly hotels or resorts that have adopted sustainable practices, such as the use of renewable energy, a reduction in water usage, and reduced waste. You can also select homestays or holiday rentals that aid local communities.

Engage in Responsible Outdoor Activities: Maui is a haven for outdoor enthusiasts, so it's crucial to use it while having as little influence as possible. Avoid engaging in activities that endanger wildlife or their habitats and opt for eco-friendly pursuits like hiking, kayaking, and snorkeling.

Supporting local communities and businesses

Supporting local organizations and companies in Maui is a fantastic way to support the local economy, advance cultural variety, and contribute to the expansion and development of the community.

Here are a few ways to help Maui's neighborhood organizations and small businesses:

Buy local: Maui is home to various small businesses, such as boutiques, marketplaces, and art galleries. You can only receive a genuine and one-of-a-kind experience by purchasing locally produced goods and helping the local economy. A great place to discover locally manufactured crafts, jewelry, and other items is at neighborhood markets like the Maui Swap Meet.

Dine local: The food scene on Maui is broad and offers everything from local cuisine to dishes from other countries. Dining at neighborhood cafes, food trucks, and restaurants is a terrific way to support the neighborhood food business and sample special meals that pay homage to the island's culture and history.

Attend Local Events: Maui has festivals and events all year long that honor everything from culture and agriculture to music and the arts. Supporting local singers and artists by attending these events allows you to discover more about Maui's distinctive traditions and culture.

Booking local excursions is a terrific way to enjoy the island's natural beauty and support the local tourism business. Maui is complete with adventure and exploration opportunities. Choose eco-friendly excursions that keep ethical travel practices and give back to the neighborhood.

Stay at Local Hostels: Local families own and run many small hotels, resorts, and vacation homes on the island of Maui. When you stay at these places, you may experience the island's distinctive culture and friendliness in addition to helping the local economy.

Volunteer: Maui's numerous nonprofit organizations and community groups rely on volunteers to fund their programs and activities. Volunteering can give back to the community and learn more about the island's history and culture.

In conclusion, contributing to the growth and development of Maui's local communities and businesses is a fantastic way to experience the island's distinctive culture and history. By favoring regional alternatives, we can support the neighborhood economy and save the island's natural beauty for upcoming generations.

CHAPTER THIRTEEN

Cultural Maui - Hawaiian cultural events and festivals

One of the finest ways to explore Hawaii's rich cultural heritage and traditions is to attend one of its many cultural events or festivals. Visitors can understand Hawaiian culture uniquely via these celebrations of everything from food and art to music and dancing. Following are a few of Hawaii's most well-known festivals and cultural events:

The Merrie Monarch Festival, which takes place in Hilo on the Big Island of Hawaii, is the most prominent hula competition in the world. It bears the name of King David Kalakaua, also referred to as the Merrie Monarch and a staunch advocate of hula.

Three days of competition are held during the festival, and hula dancers from all over the world attend to compete for prizes like Miss Aloha Hula or the group kahiko and auana hula competitions.

Hawaii Food & Wine Festival: This yearly event brings together some of the world's most well-known chefs, winemakers, and mixologists to promote Hawaii's various culinary options. It occurs on numerous islands and includes multiple activities, such as tastings, cooking demos, and VIP dinners.

Early November sees the Big Island host the Kona Coffee Culture Festival, which honors Kona's rich coffee tradition. Live music, farm visits, coffee tastings, and cultural acts are part of the festival.

Maui County Fair: This yearly event, which takes place in Wailuku, Maui, offers a selection of carnival games, rides, and food stalls. The fair also includes live entertainment, livestock shows, and cultural exhibits.

Aloha Festivals are held all around Hawaii each September as part of a month-long celebration of Hawaiian culture. The festival has many different events, such as parades, music and dance performances, and cultural exhibits.

Thousands of lanterns are floated on the waves of Ala Moana Beach Park in Honolulu as part of the annual Lantern Floating Hawaii celebration, which takes place on Memorial Day. The festival also features music, dance, and cultural acts, and the lanterns stand in for loved ones who have passed away.

Hawaii International Film Festival: This event, held in November on Oahu, features movies from the Pacific, Asia, and Hawaii. Film screenings, panel discussions, and special activities are part of the festival.

You may fully experience Hawaiian culture and discover more about the state's rich history and customs by attending these events.

Historical sites and museums

Hawaii's lovely island of Maui is home to several historical landmarks and museums where tourists may learn more about the island's fascinating past. The following list includes some of Maui's most well-known historical sites and museums:

Haleakala National Park: is a well-known tourist destination on Maui in the island's southeast. Haleakala Crater, a dormant volcano whose last eruption occurred more than 500 years ago, is in the park. To learn more about the geology and history of the island, visitors can explore the park's hiking trails, scenic roads, and visitor centers.

The Bailey House Museum: is a Wailuku institution devoted to preserving and disseminating Maui's history and culture. The museum is home to artifacts, images, and records depicting Maui's inhabitants and their way of life.

Self-guided walking tours that take tourists through the historic village of Lahaina are available on the Lahaina Heritage Trail. Sixty-two attractions along the trail include museums, historical buildings, and places of cultural relevance.

Whalers Village Museum: Located in Lahaina, this museum is devoted to preserving the past of Maui's whaling industry. The museum includes historical whaling exhibitions as well as equipment and artifact displays.

Alexander and Baldwin Sugar Museum: The history of Maui's sugar business is committed to being preserved at the Alexander and Baldwin Sugar Museum, which is situated in Puunene. The museum has exhibitions of sugar-related items and machinery and exhibits on the development and history of sugar manufacturing.

The Maui Ocean Center: is a Maalaea facility devoted to presenting Hawaii's aquatic life. The facility offers educational programs, interactive displays, and exhibits on Hawaii's coral reefs, sharks, and other marine life.

Maui's rich history and culture can be discovered by visiting these museums and historical places. Everyone may explore and learn something new on this lovely island, whether their interests are in geology, agriculture, or marine life.

Traditional arts and crafts

Hawaii's stunning island of Maui is home to a wide variety of traditional arts and crafts that showcase the island's culture and heritage. The following are a few of Maui's most well-liked traditional arts and crafts:

Making lei is a traditional art form in Hawaii that entails weaving flowers, leaves, or shells into a wreath or garland. Maui visitors have the opportunity to take part in classes where they can learn how to manufacture their own lei using conventional supplies and methods.

Hula dancing: Hula dancing is a traditional Hawaiian dance that uses hand gestures and body language to convey stories. To discover more about the origins and significance of this exquisite art form, tourists to Maui can attend hula performances and lessons.

Wood carving: Carving wooden artifacts like bowls, masks, and figures is a traditional Mauian craft known as wood carving. Visitors can buy handcrafted wooden gifts and observe talented artists at work.

Quilting: Making colorful coverlets out of fabric scraps is a traditional skill on the island of Maui. Visitors can take courses and classes in quilting to learn how to create their authentic Hawaiian quilt.

Lauhala weaving: is a traditional technique practiced on the island of Maui that entails creating mats, baskets, and hats out of dried leaves from the Hala tree. Visitors can buy handcrafted lauhala souvenirs and observe professional weavers at work.

Making ukuleles: The ukulele is a Hawaiian musical instrument with a global following. Visitors to Maui can participate in seminars to learn how to make their authentic Hawaiian ukuleles.

These traditional arts and crafts greatly influence the culture and history of Maui. By attending seminars, observing talented craftspeople at work, and purchasing handmade things as gifts, visitors to the island can fully immerse themselves in these traditions.

CHAPTER FOURTEEN.

Road Trips in Maui - West Maui Loop

The West Maui Loop is a scenic drive that takes visitors to the beautiful West Maui coastline. The loop is a 52-mile drive that starts and ends in Kahului and takes approximately two to three hours to complete, depending on how many stops you make.

The drive takes visitors through several small towns and past some of Maui's most beautiful beaches and landmarks. Some of the highlights of the West Maui Loop include:

Kaanapali Beach: Kaanapali Beach is one of Maui's most popular beaches, known for its golden sand and crystal-clear waters. The beach has hotels and resorts; visitors can enjoy swimming, snorkeling, and sunbathing.

Lahaina Town: Lahaina Town is a historic town once the Hawaiian Kingdom's capital. The city has many historic landmarks, art galleries, and restaurants. Visitors can explore the town's streets, visit the historic whaling village, and watch the sunset over the ocean.

Nakalele Blowhole: The Nakalele Blowhole is a natural wonder that shoots up to 100 feet of seawater in the air. Visitors can hike to the blowhole on the northern coast of Maui and watch as waves crash into the rocks and create an impressive spray.

Honolua Bay: Honolua Bay is a beautiful snorkeling spot on Maui's northwestern coast. The bay is home to a colorful coral reef and various marine life, including sea turtles, octopuses, and reef sharks.

Iao Valley State Park: Iao Valley State Park is a lush valley in central Maui. The park is home to the

Iao Needle, a 1,200-foot volcanic spire popular hiking destination. Visitors can explore the park's trails, learn about Hawaiian history and culture at the park's visitor center, and enjoy the scenic views of the valley.

The West Maui Loop is a must-do activity for visitors to Maui who want to experience the island's natural beauty and learn about its history and culture.

The drive offers stunning coastline views, hiking, snorkeling, and swimming opportunities, and a chance to explore some of Maui's charming towns and historic landmarks.

Upcountry Maui

Upcountry Maui is a beautiful and serene region in the heart of Maui Island, Hawaii. It is situated on the slopes of Haleakala, one of the world's largest dormant volcanoes, which towers 10,023 feet above sea level.

The region encompasses several towns, including Kula, Pukalani, and Makawao, and rolling hills, verdant pastures, and stunning panoramic views of the Pacific Ocean characterize it.

Upcountry Maui is known for its cooler temperatures, a welcome relief from the tropical heat in other parts of Maui. The area is also famous for its rich agricultural heritage and is home to several farms and ranches.

Visitors can tour the Maui Winery or the Ali'i Kula Lavender Farm, offering breathtaking views and opportunities to sample locally produced wine and lavender products.

Another popular attraction in Upcountry Maui is the Haleakala National Park, which covers over 30,000 acres of land and is home to some of the most spectacular natural wonders in the region.

Visitors can take a guided tour of the park, hike along the numerous trails, or enjoy the stunning views from one of the many lookout points.

Makawao, a charming town in Upcountry Maui, is known for its rich cultural heritage and artistic community. It is home to several art galleries and studios where visitors can view and purchase locally made artwork. The town also hosts several annual events, including the Makawao Rodeo and the Maui County Agricultural Festival.

For those looking for an authentic Hawaiian experience, Upcountry Maui offers several opportunities to experience traditional Hawaiian culture.

The region is home to several ancient Hawaiian sites, including the Piilanihale Heiau, one of Hawaii's largest surviving heiaus (Hawaiian temples).

In conclusion, Upcountry Maui is a must-visit destination for anyone looking to experience Maui's natural beauty and cultural heritage. The region offers something for everyone with its cooler temperatures, stunning views, and rich agricultural and artistic traditions.

Whether you are interested in hiking, culture, art, or simply relaxing and enjoying the breathtaking scenery, Upcountry Maui is the perfect destination.

South Maui Drive

South Maui Drive is a scenic road along the southern coast of Maui, one of the Hawaiian Islands. The drive begins in the town of Kihei and winds along the coast through the communities of Wailea and Makena, offering stunning views of the Pacific Ocean and the island's rugged shoreline.

The road is relatively short, only about 8 miles long, but it is packed with breathtaking scenery and various attractions. One of the most popular stops along the way is Wailea Beach, a long stretch of golden sand and crystal-clear water perfect for swimming, snorkeling, and sunbathing. Visitors can also enjoy the nearby Wailea Resort's amenities, including world-class restaurants, shops, and golf courses.

Another highlight of South Maui Drive is the Makena Beach State Park, located at the road's southern end. This pristine beach is a favorite spot for locals and tourists alike, and it offers a wide range of activities, such as surfing, boogie boarding, and paddle boarding.

As you drive along South Maui Drive, you will encounter several scenic overlooks offering panoramic views of the coastline and the surrounding landscape. One such overlook is Palauea Beach Park, perched on a rocky outcrop and provides a stunning vantage point for watching the waves crash against the shore.

Finally, the road ends at La Perouse Bay, a rugged and remote beach accessible only by foot. This secluded bay is excellent for hiking, snorkeling, and exploring the rocky shoreline.

Overall, South Maui Drive is a must-visit destination for anyone traveling to Maui. With its stunning beaches, world-class resorts, and breathtaking scenery, it offers a taste of the island's natural beauty and relaxed lifestyle.

East Maui Drive

East Maui Drive is a scenic road that winds along the northeastern coast of Maui, one of the Hawaiian Islands. The drive offers stunning views of the Pacific Ocean, lush rainforests, cascading waterfalls, and the towering cliffs of the island's eastern shore.

The road begins in Paia, a charming and eclectic community that is the gateway to Maui's famed North

Shore. From there, East Maui Drive takes you through several small towns and communities, each with unique characters and attractions.

One of the highlights of the drive is the town of Hana, located on the easternmost point of Maui. Hana is known for its stunning natural beauty, including the nearby Wai'anapanapa State Park, where visitors can explore black sand beaches, lava caves, and sea arches. The road to Hana is also dotted with numerous waterfalls, including the famous Seven Sacred Pools, which offer refreshing swimming opportunities.

Visitors can also stop at numerous lookout points to enjoy the spectacular coastline views and the surrounding mountains. The drive can be completed in a single day, but many visitors take their time and explore the various attractions along the way, making it a multi-day adventure.

One of the challenges of East Maui Drive is its narrow and winding roads, which require careful driving and attention to the road. However, the stunning beauty of the scenery and the numerous attractions along the way make it a must-see destination for anyone visiting Maui.

CHAPTER FIFTEEN.

Off-the-Beaten-Path in Maui - Hidden beaches and waterfalls

Maui, one of the Hawaiian Islands, is known for its beautiful beaches and breathtaking waterfalls. While some of these natural wonders are well-known and heavily visited, others are more hidden and require some effort to discover. Here are some of Maui's best-hidden beaches and waterfalls:

Red Sand Beach: Located in Hana, Red Sand Beach is a secluded cove with striking red sand, turquoise waters, and towering cliffs. Access to the beach is through a short trail that can be steep and slippery, but the reward is worth the effort.

Secret Beach: Also located in Hana, Secret Beach is a small, secluded cove with crystal-clear waters and pristine white sand. Access to the beach is through a narrow, rocky trail that can be challenging, but the beauty of the beach is well worth the effort.

Twin Falls: Twin Falls is a series of waterfalls on Maui's North Shore. The falls are easily accessible through a short hike, and visitors can swim in the pools beneath the falls.

Waimoku Falls: Located in the eastern part of Maui, Waimoku Falls is a majestic waterfall that drops 400 feet into a serene pool. Access to the falls is through a 4-mile hike, which can be challenging but offers stunning views of the surrounding landscape.

Olivine Pools: Olivine Pools are a series of natural tide pools on Maui's northwest shore. The collections are formed by lava rocks and are filled with crystal-clear seawater. Access to the pools is through a rocky trail that can be challenging, but the reward is a unique swimming experience.

Secret hikes and trails

Maui, one of the Hawaiian Islands, is known for its beautiful beaches and breathtaking waterfalls. While some of these natural wonders are well-known and heavily visited, others are more hidden and require some effort to discover. Here are some of Maui's best-hidden beaches and waterfalls:

Red Sand Beach: Located in Hana, Red Sand Beach is a secluded cove with striking red sand, turquoise waters, and towering cliffs. Access to the beach is through a short trail that can be steep and slippery, but the reward is worth the effort.

Secret Beach: Also located in Hana, Secret Beach is a small, secluded cove with crystal-clear waters and pristine white sand. Access to the beach is through a narrow, rocky trail that can be challenging, but the beauty of the beach is well worth the effort.

Twin Falls: Twin Falls is a series of waterfalls on Maui's North Shore. The falls are easily accessible through a short hike, and visitors can swim in the pools beneath the falls.

Waimoku Falls: Located in the eastern part of Maui, Waimoku Falls is a majestic waterfall that drops 400 feet into a serene pool. Access to the falls is through a 4-mile hike, which can be challenging but offers stunning views of the surrounding landscape.

Olivine Pools: Olivine Pools are a series of natural tide pools on Maui's northwest shore. The collections are formed by lava rocks and are filled with crystal-clear seawater.

Access to the pools is through a rocky trail that can be challenging, but the reward is a unique swimming experience. Maui's hidden beaches and waterfalls allow visitors to experience the island's natural beauty away from the crowds.

While some of these locations require a bit of effort to access, the reward is a peaceful and serene experience in some of the most beautiful spots on the island.

Unique cultural experiences

Maui is a melting pot of cultures influenced by Hawaiian, Polynesian, Asian, and European traditions. Visitors can immerse themselves in unique cultural experiences, from learning traditional Hawaiian crafts to exploring the island's rich history. Here are some of Maui's best cultural experiences:

Hawaiian Cultural Tours: Visitors can explore the island's rich cultural heritage through guided tours that showcase traditional Hawaiian practices, including hula dancing, lei-making, and ukulele playing. These tours offer a unique insight into the island's history and traditions.

Maui Arts and Cultural Center: The Maui Arts and Cultural Center hosts various cultural events, including music, dance, theater, and art exhibits. Visitors can experience the island's diverse cultural scene through performances by local and international artists.

Maui Ocean Center: The Maui Ocean Center offers visitors a chance to learn about the island's marine life and the cultural significance of the ocean to Hawaiian culture. Visitors can explore exhibits on marine life, including a shark tank, and learn about traditional Hawaiian fishing practices.

Road to Hana: This scenic drive takes visitors through some of Maui's most beautiful landscapes, including lush rainforests and cascading waterfalls. Visitors can explore traditional Hawaiian villages and learn about the island's history and culture.

Maui Historical Society: The Maui Historical Society preserves and celebrates the island's rich history through various exhibits and events. Visitors can explore the island's plantation era, learn about Hawaiian royalty, and discover the island's role in World War II.

CHAPTER SIXTEEN.

Maui for Adventure Seekers - Extreme sports and activities

Maui is well-known for its lovely beaches and natural scenery, but the island is also a paradise for adventure and extreme sports. Guests can test their limits with various heart-pounding activities, from skydiving and ziplining to surfing and windsurfing. The following are some of the top extreme sports and activities on Maui:

Surfing: Honolua Bay and Pe'ahi, often known as Jaws, are two of the top surfing places on Maui, which is noted for its waves. Surfers of all skill levels can find a wave to test themselves on, and for beginners, many surf schools and instructors are available.

Windsurfing: Maui is a top-notch destination thanks to its reliable trade winds and warm waters. Several of the best locations on the island, like

Ho'okipa Beach and Kanaha Beach Park, allow visitors to take lessons or rent equipment.

Skydiving: Tourists can jump out of a plane in tandem for high-octane excitement. The spectacular views of the island's mountains and shoreline provided by skydiving businesses make for a fantastic experience.

Ziplining: Maui's untamed terrain and lush rainforests combine for an exhilarating ziplining excursion. Some of the island's best zipline experiences, such as the Flyin' Hawaiian Zipline and the Kapalua Zipline, allow visitors to soar over canyons, waterfalls, and treetops.

Scuba diving: Both novice and expert divers can enjoy superb scuba diving chances in Maui's crystal clear seas. Explore the island's vivid coral reefs to see various aquatic life, including sharks, sea turtles, and vibrant fish.

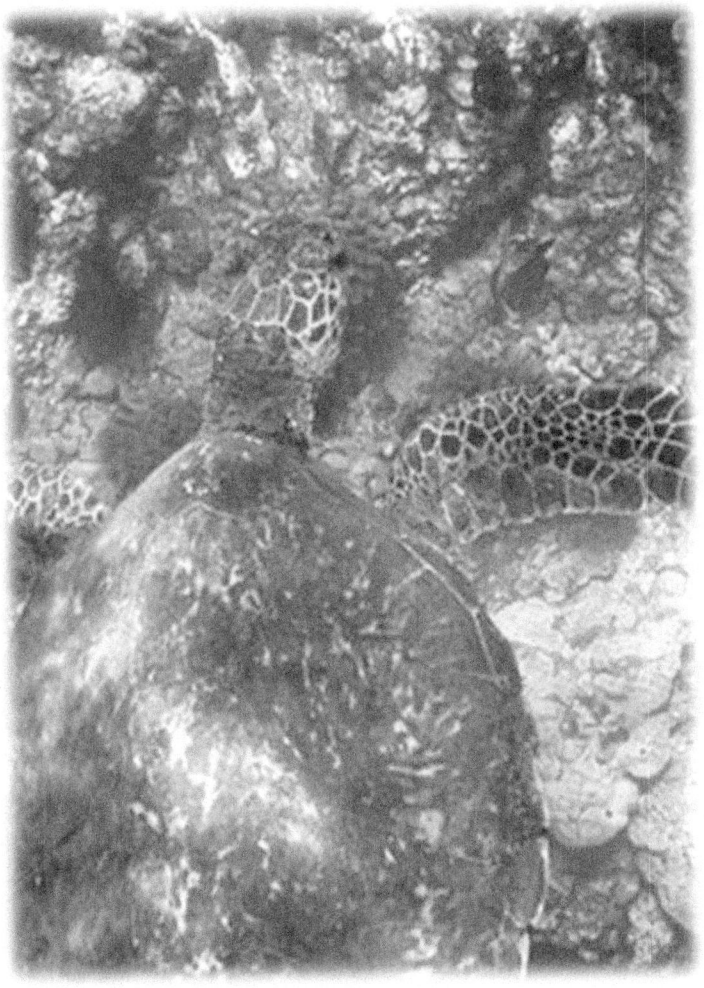

CHAPTER SEVENTEEN

Maui for Romance - Romantic activities and attractions

Maui is a romantic place with plenty of activities and attractions for couples. There is something for every team on the island, whether they are searching for excitement, relaxation, or a combination of the two. Here are some romantic things to do and places to visit in Maui:

Sunset View at Haleakal: Haleakal, a volcanic crater on the eastern side of Maui, is a great place to view the dawn or sunset. It's a common pastime to observe the sunrise or sunset from the summit for a good cause. The views are stunning, and the sky is a riot of pink, orange, and purple hues.

Take a whale-watching tour: Humpback whales can be found in Maui's seas from December to April.

Going on a whale-watching tour is a romantic way to get up and personal with these gorgeous creatures.

Drive along the Road to Hana for some breathtaking scenery: This road winds along Maui's northeastern coast. The route has waterfalls, luxuriant vegetation, and spectacular ocean views. Along the journey, you can make pit stops to check out waterfalls, hike to beaches, and eat and drink locally.

Enjoy a sunset cruise: Seeing the sunset from the ocean is an unforgettable romantic experience. Numerous businesses provide supper, cocktails, and live music sunset cruises.

Take a helicopter trip: You can take a helicopter trip to see Maui's diverse environment, which includes mountains, waterfalls, and beaches. A remarkable and romantic way to experience the island is by taking a helicopter tour.

Unwind on the beach: Maui is home to some of the world's most stunning beaches. Spend the day relaxing on the sand with a book, a towel, and sunscreen.

Have a massage together: Couples massages are available at many spas in Maui. As you both indulge in massages, facials, and other treatments, unwind and unwind together.

Take a scuba diving or snorkeling excursion: Marine life abounds in the waters off Maui, including various fish, sea turtles, and even manta rays. Together, going snorkeling or scuba diving is a romantic and enjoyable approach to discovering the underwater world.

For couples seeking a romantic trip, Maui is a great choice. There is something for every team to enjoy in this place with its breathtaking natural beauty, exciting activities, and calming attractions.

Best locations for a honeymoon

Hawaii's Maui is a stunning island perfect for honeymooners looking to enjoy adventure activities and the area's natural beauty. Here are a few of Maui's top spots for a honeymoon:

Wailea Beach, located on Maui's south coast, is one of the most beautiful beaches in the world. Swimming, snorkeling, and sunbathing are all excellent beach activities. Also, there are lots of resorts and eateries around that have top-notch feature amenities.

Haleakala National Park: The 10,023-foot-tall dormant Haleakala volcano can be found here. Couples can visit the volcano at sunrise or sunset and enjoy the breathtaking views from the top. Throughout the park, there are a lot of hiking paths that provide spectacular island views.

Kaanapali Beach: On Maui's west coast is a beach called Kaanapali Beach, renowned for its silky sand and crystal-clear seas. Swimming, snorkeling, and sunset sailboat tours are activities couples can enjoy together.

Lahaina: On Maui's west coast, in the town of Lahaina, there are numerous art galleries, stores, and dining establishments. Couples can savor the local food while strolling the town's streets.

Intimate dining experiences

Maui is a magnificent island in Hawaii known for its breathtaking beaches, natural surroundings, and energetic culture. The island's outstanding culinary culture, which offers various eating options to suit every taste and budget, is one of its best-kept secrets. This post will concentrate on secluded dining locales in Maui that will provide you with priceless recollections.

Private Chef Experience

A private chef experience is one of Maui's most private dining occasions. Some seasoned chefs provide individualized dining experiences where they design a menu specifically for you and your group.

The chef will prepare a gourmet meal in your villa or hotel room, offering a really exclusive and private dining experience. Couples seeking a romantic evening or a small group of friends commemorating a particular event would find this encounter ideal.

Dinner cruise at dusk

A sunset dinner boat in Maui is yet another wonderful exclusive dining occasion. Several businesses offer private or semi-private dinner cruises, giving stunning views of the island's coastline and sunset. A gourmet meal and drinks are typically provided on dinner cruises, making them ideal for commemorating a special occasion or spending a romantic evening with your significant other.

Farm-to-Table Dining

Farm-to-table dining is a well-liked culinary trend in Maui due to the island's abundance of local farms and fresh vegetables. Several eateries provide farm-to-table dining experiences, where the chef designs the menu using only the finest local products.

You may savor delectable seasonal cuisine while promoting local farmers and sustainable agriculture at these quaint dining establishments.

Experience at the Chef's Table

Consider scheduling a chef's table experience if you want a genuinely exclusive and private eating experience. Many restaurants let you sit at the chef's table and watch them create your food.

You can interact directly with the chef during this eating experience, ask them questions, and discover more about the cooking methods that went into making your dish.

CHAPTER EIGHTEEN

Maui for Solo Travelers Solo - friendly activities and events.

Maui offers plenty to everyone, whether they are looking for adventure, relaxation, or cultural immersion. These are some Maui activities and events that are suitable for lone travelers:

Take a hike: Maui offers a selection of routes for hikers of all experience levels. The Waihee Ridge Trail, Iao Valley State Park, and Haleakala National Park are well-liked possibilities. Go hiking to discover Maui's natural beauty, exercise, and meet other lone travelers.

Attend a luau: A Maui must-do is to take part in a traditional Hawaiian luau. You may eat delectable food, take in hula performances, and discover Hawaiian culture.

The Old Lahaina Luau, the Feast at Lele, and the Drums of the Ocean Luau are a few of the well-known luaus in Maui.

Visit the Maui Ocean Center: This educational facility is an excellent spot to learn about Hawaii's marine biodiversity. Many species, such as sharks, sea turtles, and tropical fish, are visible. Moreover, the institution provides tours and educational events.

Take a snorkeling or diving vacation: Maui features some of Hawaii's top locations for these activities. You can view aquatic life, swim with sea turtles, and explore vibrant coral reefs. Some well-known places are Molokini Crater, Honolua Bay, and the Ahihi Kinau Natural Area Reserve.

Take a yoga or meditation lesson: Maui is renowned for its offers in these areas. Numerous yoga and meditation classes are available for people of various experience levels. Maui Yoga Shala, Maui Hot Yoga, and Maui Healing Retreat are well-known studios.

Take a Scenic drive: Maui offers some of Hawaii's most stunning scenery. You can rent a car and go for a beautiful drive along the Kahekili Highway or the Road to Hana. You can pause along the route at waterfalls, beaches, and other picturesque locations.

Visit a farmers market: Fresh vegetables, baked products, and handcrafted crafts are available at Maui's many farmer's markets. The Upcountry Farmers Market, the Napili Farmers Market, and the Maui Swap Meet are well-known markets.

All in all, Maui has a selection of solo-friendly events and activities that cater to various interests and preferences. You'll definitely find something here, no matter what you're looking for—adventure, relaxation, or cultural immersion.

Social and networking opportunities

Maui, the second-largest island in Hawaii, is a great destination for social and networking opportunities.

Whether you are a solo traveler, a business professional, or someone looking to expand your social circle, Maui offers a variety of options to connect with others.

Here are some social and networking opportunities in Maui to consider:

Attend a Chamber of Commerce event: The Maui Chamber of Commerce hosts a variety of events throughout the year, including mixers, luncheons, and workshops. These events provide a great opportunity to network with other professionals and learn about local businesses.

Join a business association: Maui has several business associations, such as the Maui Native Hawaiian Chamber of Commerce and the Hawaii Women's Business Center. These associations offer networking events, business resources, and educational opportunities for their members.

Attend a cultural event: Maui has a rich cultural heritage that is celebrated through various events throughout the year. You can attend a hula festival, a lei-making workshop, or a traditional Hawaiian music performance. These events provide an opportunity to connect with others who share an interest in Hawaiian culture.

Join a social club: Maui has several social clubs that cater to different interests, such as hiking, kayaking, and photography. These clubs offer a great opportunity to meet other people who share your passions and explore Maui's natural beauty.

Attend a meetup: Meetup is a popular platform that connects people with similar interests in their local area. You can join a meetup group for hiking, photography, or any other interest you have and attend events to meet other like-minded individuals.

Volunteer: Maui has several nonprofit organizations that are always looking for volunteers. You can volunteer at a local animal shelter, beach cleanup, or food bank. Not only will you be helping the community, but you'll also have the opportunity to meet other volunteers who share your passion for making a difference.

Overall, Maui offers a variety of social and networking opportunities for people of all ages and interests. Whether you're looking to connect with other professionals, learn about Hawaiian culture, or meet new friends, there are plenty of options to choose from in Maui.

Safety tips for solo travelers

Attend a Maui Chamber of Commerce event: The Maui Chamber of Commerce organizes several events all year long, such as mixers, luncheons, and workshops. These gatherings offer a fantastic chance to network with other professionals and discover local businesses.

Join a business organization: Maui is home to several organizations, including the Hawaii Women's Business Center and the Maui Native Hawaiian Chamber of Commerce. These organizations provide their members with networking possibilities, business resources, and educational opportunities.

Attend a cultural event: Various activities honor Maui's rich cultural legacy year-round. You can go to a lei-making class, a hula festival, or a concert of Hawaiian music. These gatherings give people a chance to meet others who are passionate about Hawaiian culture.

Join a social club: Some social groups on Maui cater to various interests, including photography, kayaking, and hiking. These groups provide an excellent way to discover Maui's natural beauty and connect with others who share your interests.

Join a meetup: Meetup is a well-known platform that brings together locals with like-minded interests. You can attend events to meet other like-minded people by joining a meeting group for hiking, photography, or any other passion you may have.

Volunteer: Several charitable groups in Maui are constantly asking for help. You can offer your time to a neighborhood food bank, beach clean-up, or animal shelter.

You'll not only be giving back to the community but also get to know other volunteers who share your enthusiasm for making a difference.

Maui provides people of all ages and interests with various social and networking possibilities. Maui offers many opportunities, whether you want to network with other professionals, discover Hawaiian culture, or make new friends.

Advice on safety for lone travelers

Like any other tourist destination, Maui necessitates that solitary travelers take specific safety measures to secure their safety.

Here are some safety recommendations for Maui solo travelers:

Before making a reservation, research the area and read reviews from prior visitors. Consider staying at a hotel or renting a vacation home that is secure and situated in a safe neighborhood.

Observe your surroundings: When you're out and about, pay attention to your surroundings and stay away from walking alone in strange or desolate regions, incredibly late at night. Keep to well-lit areas and refrain from bringing expensive items with you.

Use reliable public transportation or rent a car to go around Maui; it's a big island, so having a rental car is recommended. Choose trustworthy transportation options like taxis, Uber, or Lyft if you don't want to hire a car.

Keep your personal property Safe: Keep your credit cards, cash, passport, and other documents safe.

Use due care: While engaging with locals, use common sense, especially if someone you don't know approaches you. Don't give your itinerary or provide personal information to strangers; instead, be courteous but cautious.

Prepare for outdoor activities: Hiking, swimming, and snorkeling are just a few of the island of Maui's famed outdoor pursuits. Take the appropriate measures and study potential risks before participating in any outdoor activity. For instance, wear proper footwear, pack lots of water and snacks, and never swim alone.

Keep up with the weather: Maui is susceptible to rapid atmospheric shifts, especially during the winter. Keep up with the weather and be ready for any potential emergencies.

These safety recommendations can help solitary visitors have a secure and happy journey to Maui. Remember that while traveling alone, safety should always come first.

CHAPTER NINTEEN.

Events and Festivals in Maui - Maui Film Festival

An annual occasion on the Hawaiian island of Maui is the Maui Film Festival. The festival honors the craft of filmmaking and presents a wide selection of movies from around the globe. These are some details regarding the Maui Film Festival:

History:

The Maui Film Festival was founded in 2000 by Barry Rivers, a filmmaker and longtime resident of Maui. The festival's mission is to celebrate cinema and promote the art of filmmaking.

The festival has since grown into one of the most popular cultural events in Maui, attracting visitors from around the world.

Events:

There are screenings, talks, and special occasions during the Maui Film Festival. Often lasting a few days, the festival offers many films, including feature-length productions, documentaries, and short films.

The festival holds various unique events in addition to movie screenings, including filmmaker forums, actor and director Q&A sessions, and film-related lectures.

Locations:

The Maui Film Festival occurs at various locations throughout Maui, including outdoor venues such as the Celestial Cinema and the Toes in the Sand Cinema. These venues provide a unique and memorable movie-going experience for festival attendees.

Awards:

The Maui Film Festival presents several yearly awards, including the Audience and Visionary awards.

The festival also honors notable filmmakers and actors with the Rainmaker and Navigator Awards.

Community Involvement:

The Maui Film Festival is deeply involved in the local community, working with local businesses and organizations to promote cultural and environmental sustainability. The festival also provides local filmmakers and actors opportunities to showcase their work.

Maui County Fair

The Maui County Fair is an annual event on the island of Maui, Hawaii. The fair is a popular cultural event that celebrates the island's heritage and offers a variety of activities for visitors of all ages.

Here is some information about the Maui County Fair:

History:

The Maui County Fair has been a tradition on the island since 1916. It was initially created to celebrate the end of the sugar cane harvest and has since become a beloved cultural event that draws visitors from around the world.

Events:

The Maui County Fair features a variety of events and activities, including livestock exhibits, carnival rides, live entertainment, and food vendors. The fair also hosts several contests, such as pie-eating contests, hula competitions, and flower shows.

Locations:

The Maui County Fair takes place at the War Memorial Complex in Wailuku. This sprawling venue features several exhibit halls, outdoor stages, and carnival rides, making it the perfect location for the fair.

Food:

The food is one of the Maui County Fair's most well-liked features. Local staples, including malasadas, spam musubi, and shaved ice, are available for tourists. Various food vendors selling everything from fried chicken to cotton candy are also at the fair.

Entertainment: The Maui County Fair offers a wide range of live entertainment, including performances by local musicians and dancers. The fair also hosts a talent show featuring local performers of all ages.

Community Involvement:

The Maui County Fair is deeply involved in the local community, working with local organizations and businesses to promote cultural awareness and sustainability. The fair also provides local vendors and artisans opportunities to showcase their work.

Whale Day Festival

The Whale Day Festival is an annual event in Maui, Hawaii. The festival celebrates the humpback whales that migrate to Maui's warm waters each winter to breed and give birth. Here is some information about the Whale Day Festival:

History:

The Whale Day Festival was first held in 1980 by the Pacific Whale Foundation, a nonprofit organization focused on protecting whales and their ocean habitat. The festival was created to raise awareness about the humpback whales migrating to Maui yearly.

Events:

The Whale Day Festival features a variety of events and activities, including live music, food vendors, children's activities, and educational exhibits. The festival also hosts a parade featuring colorful floats and costumes.

Locations:

The Whale Day Festival occurs at Kalama Park in Kihei, Maui. This beautiful beachfront park provides the perfect backdrop for the festival's activities.

Whale Watching:

In addition to the festival's events, visitors can also participate in whale-watching tours. The humpback whales are a festival highlight, and visitors can get up close and personal with these majestic creatures on guided tours.

Education:

The Whale Day Festival is also an educational event, teaching visitors about humpback whales and their importance to the ocean ecosystem. The festival features educational exhibits, presentations, and guided walks.

Community Involvement:

The Whale Day Festival is deeply involved in the local community, working with local businesses and organizations to promote environmental sustainability and cultural awareness.

Maui Marathon

The Maui Marathon is an annual event held on the beautiful island of Maui in Hawaii. The marathon takes place in early October and is a popular event for runners worldwide looking for a challenging and scenic race.

The Maui Marathon is a 26.2-mile race that starts at the Sugar Beach Resort in Kihei and finishes at the Kaanapali Beach Resort.

The race course follows the stunning coastline of Maui, passing through small towns, lush green forests, and along the oceanfront.

The race is organized by the Maui Marathon Foundation, a non-profit organization committed to promoting health and fitness in the community.

The foundation has been organizing the event since 1971 and has a reputation for providing runners of all levels with a well-organized and enjoyable race experience.

In addition to the full marathon, the Maui Marathon also offers a half marathon, a 10K race, and a 5K race, so runners of all abilities can participate in the event. The races are timed, and runners receive a finisher medal and t-shirt upon completion.

One of the highlights of the Maui Marathon is the stunning scenery along the racecourse. Runners pass by palm trees, crystal clear water, and scenic vistas that will take their breath away.

The course is relatively flat, with a few rolling hills, so it is considered a fast and accessible race for runners of all abilities.

The Maui Marathon is more than just a race; it also celebrates Hawaiian culture and tradition. The event includes a pre-race ceremony and a post-race party, where runners can enjoy live music, Hawaiian food, and refreshments.

Slack Key Guitar Festival

The Slack Key Guitar Festival in Maui is an annual music event celebrating the Hawaiian slack key guitar's unique and soulful sound.

The festival is held in various locations throughout Maui and features performances by some of the world's most talented sloppy critical guitarists. The slack key guitar is a style of playing the guitar that originated in Hawaii in the 19th century.

The technique involves loosening or "slacking" the guitar strings to create a more resonant and melodic sound. The result is a beautiful, soulful sound instantly recognizable and deeply rooted in Hawaiian culture.

The Slack Key Guitar Festival in Maui celebrates this distinctive style of guitar playing. The festival typically takes place over several days and features performances by some of the world's most respected and renowned slack critical guitarists. The festival also includes workshops, lectures, and other events designed to educate visitors about the history and culture of the Hawaiian slack key guitar.

One of the highlights of the Slack Key Guitar Festival is the intimate and personal atmosphere of the performances. Unlike more prominent music festivals, the Slack Key Guitar Festival is designed to be a more intimate and personal experience, with small venues and an emphasis on connecting with the artists and the music.

The festival also provides a unique opportunity for visitors to experience Hawaiian culture and hospitality. In addition to the music, the festival typically includes food, drink, and other cultural events, providing an authentic taste of Hawaiian hospitality and tradition.

Overall, the Slack Key Guitar Festival in Maui is a must-see event for anyone who loves music, culture, and the beauty of Hawaii. With its world-class performers, intimate venues, and deep connection to Hawaiian culture, it is a unique and unforgettable experience that is not to be missed.

CHAPTER TWENTY

Travel Tips for Maui - Money-saving tips.

Maui is a beautiful and popular tourist destination known for its beaches, water sports, and scenic landscapes. However, like most tourist destinations, it can also be expensive. To help you extend your holiday budget when visiting Maui, consider the following money-saving advice:

Travel during the off-season: Maui's peak tourist season is during the summer and winter holidays, so traveling during the off-season (spring or fall) can save you money on airfare, accommodations, and activities.

Book early: Booking your flights, accommodations, and activities in advance can often save you money, especially if you are flexible with your travel dates.

Consider alternative accommodations: While Maui has plenty of luxury resorts, there are also more affordable options like vacation rentals, hostels, and camping grounds. Consider staying in a condo or Airbnb to save money by cooking meals.

Look for free activities: Maui has plenty of free activities, such as hiking trails, beaches, and parks. Spend your days exploring the island's natural beauty without spending a dime.

Rent a car: Renting a car can be more cost-effective than taking taxis or private tours, especially if you plan to explore the island independently.

Bring your snacks and drinks: Buying snacks and drinks at convenience stores or tourist spots can quickly add up. Bring your snacks and drinks to save money and avoid unnecessary expenses.

Use coupons and discounts: Look for coupons and discounts for activities, restaurants, and shops in Maui. You can often find deals on local tourist guides or online.

Take advantage of happy hour specials: Many restaurants and bars in Maui offer happy hour specials, which can save you money on food and drinks.

Skip the souvenirs: Souvenirs can be expensive, especially if you buy them at tourist shops. Consider skipping the souvenirs altogether or buying them at local markets or thrift shops.

Following these money-saving tips can make the most of your Maui vacation without breaking the bank.

Safety and health tips

Maui is a beautiful Hawaii island known for its stunning beaches, breathtaking landscapes, and diverse culture. Whether you're a resident or a visitor, it's essential to prioritize safety and health to ensure an enjoyable and safe experience. Keep the following tips in mind:

Stay Hydrated: The tropical climate of Maui can be hot and humid, leading to dehydration. It's crucial to drink plenty of water and stay hydrated throughout the day, especially if you're spending time outdoors.

Protect Yourself from the Sun: The sun's rays can be intense in Maui, and prolonged exposure can lead to sunburn, skin damage, and even skin cancer. Use sunscreen with an SPF of 30 or higher, wear a hat and sunglasses, and seek shade during the day's hottest hours.

Watch out for Ocean Hazards: Maui's beaches are a significant draw for visitors but can also be hazardous. Always follow posted signs, avoid swimming alone, and be mindful of rip currents, which can quickly pull you out to sea.

Be Prepared for Hiking: Maui has some incredible hiking trails, but they can be challenging, especially if unprepared. Wear sturdy shoes, bring plenty of water and snacks, and tell someone where you're going and when you expect to return.

Be Cautious of Wildlife: Maui is home to a diverse array of wildlife, including sea turtles, whales, and sharks. Always maintain a safe distance, never feed or touch the animals, and respect their natural habitat.

Practice Safe Driving: If renting a car or driving in Maui, be aware of the unique driving conditions, such as narrow, winding roads and steep hills. Follow the speed limit, wear your seatbelt, and avoid distracted driving.

Follow COVID-19 Guidelines: As with the rest of the world, Maui is also facing the COVID-19 pandemic. Follow the local guidelines on masks, social distancing, and vaccination requirements to keep yourself and others safe.

Language and cultural tips

Maui is a unique and diverse destination with a rich cultural history. Here are some language and cultural tips to keep in mind when visiting or interacting with the local community:

Respect Hawaiian Culture: It is an essential part of Maui's identity, and it's vital to respect it. Learn about Hawaiian history and culture, and be mindful of sacred places, such as heiaus and burial sites.

Use the Hawaiian Language: The Hawaiian language is an official language in Hawaii, and it's always appreciated when visitors try to use Hawaiian words and phrases. Learn essential words and phrases like "aloha" (hello/goodbye), "mahalo" (thank you), and "'ohana" (family).

Be Punctual: Being on time is highly valued in Hawaiian culture. Arriving late for a meeting or event can be seen as disrespectful.

Dress Appropriately: Hawaiian culture values modesty, so it's essential to dress appropriately. Avoid wearing revealing clothing in public areas and wear appropriate attire when visiting sacred sites.

Practice Respectful Behavior: Hawaiian culture values humility, kindness, and respect. Be polite, and respect locals and their customs.

Be Open to Learning: Hawaii has a diverse community, and learning about different cultures and traditions can be a rich experience. Be open-minded and willing to learn about the different cultures represented on the island.

Participate in Cultural Activities: Maui offers various cultural activities, including hula shows, lei-making workshops, and cultural festivals. Take part in these events to experience and learn about Hawaiian culture.

In summary, Maui has a rich cultural history, and visitors should respect local customs and traditions. Use the Hawaiian language, dress appropriately, be punctual, practice respectful behavior, be open to learning, and participate in cultural activities. By embracing these tips, visitors can enhance their experience on the island and contribute to preserving Hawaiian culture.

Made in the USA
Middletown, DE
21 January 2024

48270583R00116